TABLE OF CONTENTS

NOTE TO READER

Financial Warnings and Disclaimer

Welcome to *From Ground Up: A Financial Empowerment for African Migrants in Australia.* This book provides general financial information and practical advice drawn from the personal experiences and knowledge of the author, Yong Deng Dau. While every effort has been made to ensure the accuracy and relevance of the content, please note that this book does not constitute personalized financial advice.

This book is intended solely for informational purposes and should not be construed as legal, financial, or tax advice. The author and publisher disclaim any liability for financial decisions or actions taken by readers based on the information presented herein.

Understanding the Nature of Financial Information

1. **General Information Only:**
   This book aims to provide a general understanding of financial concepts, strategies, and practices. It is designed to help you navigate the Australian financial system and offers insights into key areas of personal finance, including budgeting, saving, investing, debt management, and retirement planning. However, financial situations differ from person to person. The advice and strategies presented here may not suit everyone and should be adapted to your unique circumstances.

2. **Not a Substitute for Professional Advice:**
   The content of this book should not replace professional financial advice. Your financial decisions should be based on a thorough assessment of your personal circumstances, goals, and risk tolerance.

It is highly recommended to consult with a certified financial advisor, tax professional, or other relevant experts before making significant financial decisions or implementing any strategies discussed in this book.

Limitations and Risks

1. **Potential Financial Risks:**
   The financial strategies and investments discussed in this book carry varying degrees of risk. Investments can fluctuate in value, and past performance does not guarantee future results. It is essential to fully understand the risks involved in any financial decision or investment and make informed choices based on your financial goals and risk tolerance.

2. **Accuracy of Information:**
   Although every effort has been made to ensure that the information provided is accurate and up to date, financial regulations, laws, and market conditions are subject to change. The information in this book may become outdated or may not reflect recent developments. Always verify current financial regulations and seek updated information from reliable sources.

Personal Responsibility

1. **Due Diligence:**
   It is your responsibility to perform due diligence and thorough research when applying the information and strategies outlined in this book. Evaluate your personal financial situation, seek professional advice when necessary, and make decisions based on a comprehensive analysis of your unique circumstances.

2. **Implementation of Strategies:**
   When implementing financial strategies, exercise caution and consider your specific situation. Financial planning involves various

factors, including income, expenses, assets, liabilities, and future goals. Ensure that you account for all these factors when applying the advice and strategies discussed in this book.

Professional Guidance

1. **Consulting Experts:**
   Financial professionals—including financial advisors, tax advisors, investment specialists, and legal experts—can offer personalized advice tailored to your specific needs. Engaging with qualified professionals can help you navigate complex financial matters, comply with regulations, and effectively achieve your financial goals.

2. **Seeking Support:**
   If you encounter financial difficulties or require assistance with financial planning, consider reaching out to financial counseling services or community organizations. These resources can provide valuable support in managing debt, budgeting, and planning for your financial future.

Empowerment Through Financial Knowledge

By choosing to engage with the principles in this book, you are taking an important and empowering step toward financial independence. Remember, learning about financial management is an act of empowerment, and applying this knowledge will help you create the financial future you envision. This book is meant to support and uplift you, no matter where you are on your financial journey. You are capable of navigating the financial challenges you may face, and with the right tools and guidance, you can take control of your financial destiny.

Inclusivity and Adaptability

Whether you're at the beginning of your financial journey or further along, From Ground Up is designed to be adaptable to different life stages and financial levels. The strategies shared in this book can be applied whether you are starting from a place of financial insecurity or already have a strong financial foundation. Remember, financial empowerment is for everyone, and this book is here to guide you at every step.

Cultural Sensitivity

As an African migrant in Australia, you may encounter unique challenges that require a culturally sensitive approach to financial planning. This book acknowledges these challenges and encourages you to seek out professionals who understand your cultural context and can provide advice that resonates with your personal experiences. Cultural nuances often influence financial decisions, and it's important to find guidance that respects and reflects your background.

Acknowledgments

Yong Deng Dau acknowledges the invaluable contributions of financial experts, resources, and institutions that informed and supported the creation of this book. The insights and advice shared are based on the author's personal experiences and knowledge in the field of finance. Yong appreciates the support of readers and encourages them to seek professional guidance to complement the information provided in this book.

Final Thoughts

The journey to financial stability and success is deeply personal, and there is no one-size-fits-all solution. Use this book as a starting point for your financial education and planning. Embrace the principles and strategies discussed, tailor them to your situation, and seek professional guidance as needed. Remember, financial literacy is an ongoing journey, and we encourage you to continue expanding your knowledge and adapting to the ever-evolving financial landscape.

Your financial well-being is a vital part of your overall quality of life. Taking proactive steps to manage your finances can lead to greater security, peace of mind, and fulfillment.

Thank you for choosing *From Ground Up: A Financial Empowerment for African Migrants in Australia.* May this guide serve as a valuable resource on your path to financial empowerment and success.

EMPOWERING FINANCIAL FUTURES: A FOREWORD BY GEORGE GIRDLER

In an ever-evolving financial landscape, the journey from uncertainty to stability and prosperity is one that many individuals and families embark on with varying degrees of success. For African migrants in Australia, this journey is filled with unique challenges and opportunities. Navigating a different cultural and economic environment requires resilience, knowledge, and strategic financial planning. It is with great pleasure and a deep sense of responsibility that I present this foreword for *From Ground Up: A Financial Empowerment for African Migrants in Australia,* authored by Yong Deng Dau.

A Personal and Professional Journey

I have had the privilege of working alongside Yong Deng Dau for many years, witnessing firsthand his resilience, commitment, and deep passion for financial literacy. Yong's story is one of remarkable determination and transformation. Arriving in Australia as a young South Sudanese man at a formative age, Yong faced the challenges of adapting to a new culture, language, and financial system. His journey is a testament to the strength, courage, and perseverance required to succeed in a new country where the rules of life—both social and economic—are vastly different from those he left behind.

Yong's personal experiences fueled his desire to help others navigate the complexities of finance. His journey from migrant to a successful professional in the Banking and Financial Services industry reflects not only his personal growth but also his commitment to giving back to the community. His career, spanning over a decade, has taken him from lending roles to business Analysis responsibilities and now to his current role as a Consultant in Data & Analytics at one of Australia's top four banks. Yong's professional journey offers invaluable insights into the financial system and its intricacies, insights that are woven throughout this book.

One thing that has always impressed me about Yong is his ability to relate to others and offer practical advice grounded in real-life experience. I've seen him sit down with individuals, listen to their challenges, and offer personalized guidance that truly makes a difference. Yong understands the power of financial literacy—not just as a tool for personal success, but as a way to uplift entire communities.

A Guide Rooted in Experience and Expertise

From Ground Up is more than just a financial guide; it is a beacon of hope and practical wisdom for African migrants seeking to understand and master the financial challenges they encounter in Australia. This book is meticulously crafted to address the specific needs of its audience, drawing on Yong's extensive experience and personal journey. Each chapter is designed to provide not only foundational knowledge but also actionable strategies that can be applied to real-life situations.

The content reflects a deep understanding of the financial obstacles and opportunities that African migrants face. Yong has thoughtfully included practical advice on a wide range of topics, from budgeting and saving to investing, managing debt, and planning for the future. For example, detailed budgeting strategies can be found on page 25, offering readers practical tools to manage their daily finances, while real estate investment guidance is available on page 129, helping readers understand the complexities of property markets in Australia. His ability to demystify complex financial concepts and present them in an accessible and engaging manner is truly commendable.

But this book goes beyond just financial advice. It's about empowerment— giving readers the tools they need to take control of their financial destinies.

Yong understands that financial literacy is not a one-size-fits-all approach, and he has tailored his advice to speak directly to the experiences of African migrants, making this guide both relatable and practical.

A Resource for Empowerment and Growth

In today's world, financial literacy is more crucial than ever. It empowers individuals to make informed decisions, achieve their financial goals, and secure their futures. For African migrants in Australia, having a resource that speaks directly to their experiences and challenges is invaluable. This book serves as that resource, offering guidance and support to those who are building their financial lives from the ground up.

Yong's dedication to financial education shines through every page of this guide. His commitment to helping others navigate the financial system with confidence and competence is a reflection of his own journey and success. He knows firsthand the importance of making sound financial decisions and the impact they can have on one's life and future. From understanding superannuation and taxes to creating an estate plan and ensuring that your legacy is protected, *From Ground Up* covers the essential aspects of financial planning that every migrant should be aware of.

This book is not just a reflection of Yong's expertise but also a manifestation of his desire to give back to the community. By sharing his knowledge, experiences, and strategies, Yong is helping others achieve their financial aspirations, build security for their families, and contribute positively to their new home in Australia.

Encouragement for the Reader

As you embark on your journey through the pages of this book, I encourage you to approach the content with an open mind and a willingness to learn. The strategies and insights presented are designed to empower you to take control of your financial future. Whether you are just beginning your financial journey or looking to refine your existing strategies, this guide offers practical advice and valuable information tailored to your needs.

As you work through each chapter, reflect on how the advice can be applied to your personal situation. Implementing even small steps can lead to significant progress in achieving financial stability. Financial success is not achieved overnight, but with perseverance, planning, and the right knowledge, it is attainable.

This book is more than a guide—it's a call to action. It's an invitation to take charge of your financial future, to build a legacy for your family, and to contribute to the broader community. Financial literacy is not just about managing money—it's about creating opportunities, securing your future, and achieving your dreams.

In Closing

I commend Yong Deng Dau for his remarkable work and unwavering commitment to financial literacy and empowerment. *From Ground Up* is a testament to his expertise and a gift to those who seek to build a secure and prosperous financial future. Financial literacy is more than just knowledge— it's empowerment. It's the confidence to navigate life's financial challenges, the wisdom to build a secure future, and the freedom to pursue your dreams with clarity and purpose.

May this book serve as a guiding light on your path to financial success and stability. Embrace the lessons within, apply them to your life, and let your financial journey be one of empowerment, growth, and lasting impact. With the right knowledge and determination, you have the power to shape your future and the future of those who come after you.

Sincerely,
George Girdler
Professional Mentor and Advisor
23 August 2024

ACKNOWLEDGMENTS

A Journey of Support and Collaboration

Writing From Ground Up: A Financial Empowerment for African Migrants in Australia was a monumental task, and it would not have been possible without the unwavering support, guidance, and encouragement of many individuals and organizations. This project reflects the collective effort of many, and I am profoundly grateful to all who contributed to its creation and success.

Special Thanks

1. **To My Family:**

   My deepest gratitude goes to my family, whose unwavering support has been the cornerstone of this journey. Your belief in my vision and constant encouragement provided the strength and motivation needed to complete this book. To my parents, thank you for your sacrifices and for instilling in me the values of perseverance and hard work. To my siblings, your love and support have been invaluable, fueling my commitment to helping others through this work.

2. **To My Mentors and Colleagues:**

   I extend heartfelt thanks to my mentors and colleagues in the Banking and Financial Services industry. Your guidance, wisdom, and expertise were instrumental in shaping my understanding of the financial system and refining the content of this book. A special acknowledgment goes to George Girdler, whose mentorship has guided me throughout my professional journey. Your feedback and encouragement have enriched this project immensely.

3. **To Financial Professionals and Experts:**

   A sincere thank you to the financial professionals who generously contributed their insights and expertise. Your input ensured that the advice and strategies presented in this book are both practical and aligned with current financial practices. Your dedication to financial literacy and your willingness to share your knowledge have made this book a stronger resource for readers.

4. **To Community Organizations and Support Groups:**

   I am deeply grateful to the African Communities Council of Australia, the African Australian Advocacy Centre, and other community organizations that support African migrants in navigating the challenges of settling in Australia. Your tireless efforts have been a source of inspiration, and I hope this book complements your work by providing additional resources and guidance for financial empowerment.

5. **To the Readers:**

   To all the readers who have chosen to embark on this journey with me, I am profoundly grateful for your trust and interest. This book is written with the hope of empowering you with the knowledge and tools needed to successfully navigate the financial landscape in Australia. Your commitment to improving your financial literacy and planning for the future is the ultimate reward for this endeavor.

Acknowledging the Role of Financial Education

Financial education is a powerful tool for empowering individuals and communities. This book reflects the collective effort of many people and organizations dedicated to enhancing financial literacy and supporting African migrants in Australia. The knowledge and insights shared within these pages are the result of years of experience, collaboration, and a shared commitment to fostering financial well-being.

I extend my gratitude to everyone who has dedicated their careers to improving financial literacy within our communities. Your work has had a lasting impact on countless lives, and this book is a humble contribution to that ongoing effort. Together, we are building a stronger, more financially empowered community.

Final Thoughts

As we move forward, I hope that From Ground Up serves as a valuable resource and guide for anyone seeking to understand and master their finances. The journey to financial stability and success is ongoing, and this book is intended to be a starting point for your financial education. Remember, financial empowerment is a continuous process, and with each step, you are investing in a brighter, more secure future for yourself and your loved ones.

Thank you once again to everyone who contributed to this project. Your support has been instrumental in making this book a reality, and I am deeply appreciative of each and every one of you.

With heartfelt thanks,
Yong Deng Dau
23 August 2024

INTRODUCTION

Welcome to *From Ground Up: A Financial Empowerment for African Migrants in Australia.* This book is more than just a guide—it's a bridge between where you are now and the financial future you've always envisioned. As you turn these pages, you will not only learn about the Australian financial system, but you will also find the motivation, strength, and confidence to seize the opportunities that lie ahead.

Why This Book?

Relocating to a new country is filled with possibilities, but it also brings challenges that can feel overwhelming—especially when it comes to managing your finances. For many African migrants, navigating Australia's financial landscape can be daunting. The systems here may feel unfamiliar, the rules complex, and the opportunities seem distant. But they don't have to be.

This book was born out of the recognition that understanding and adapting to Australia's financial system is crucial for achieving stability, security, and success. Whether you are sending money home to support family, saving to buy your first home, or planning for retirement, this guide is crafted to help you demystify these complexities, take control of your financial destiny, and transform your life through informed decisions.

Purpose and Scope

From Ground Up is not just a financial guide—it is your partner in building a new life in Australia. Whether you're just starting or have been here for some time, this book provides the tools, insights, and strategies necessary for managing your finances effectively. It covers everything from budgeting and saving to investing and retirement planning, ensuring that you are well-equipped for every financial decision that comes your way.

Each chapter stands alone, offering practical advice that you can immediately apply to your life. Whether you're managing your first paycheck, buying a home, or planning for retirement, this book will guide you every step of the way.

What You Will Learn

This book is divided into ten chapters, each focusing on a key area of financial management:

1. **Understanding the Financial System in Australia**
   Learn how the Australian financial system operates and gain the foundational knowledge you need to navigate it with confidence.

2. **Budgeting and Financial Planning**
   Discover practical strategies for budgeting, controlling expenses, and reaching your financial goals.

3. **Understanding Credit and Loans**
   Understand credit, improve your credit score, and make smart borrowing decisions.

4. **Investing for the Future**
   Explore options for saving and investing, from building an emergency fund to creating long-term wealth through investments.

5. **Managing Debt**
   Learn strategies to effectively manage debt, avoid pitfalls, and maintain a healthy financial balance.

6. **Saving for Major Life Goals**

    Learn how to set savings goals for significant life events, such as buying a home, funding education, or starting a business.

7. **Understanding and Managing Taxes**

    Get clear on your tax obligations, deductions, and strategies for maximising your returns.

8. **Retirement Planning, Superannuation, and Estate Planning**

    Secure your future by understanding superannuation, retirement planning, and estate planning strategies.

9. **Navigating Financial Challenges and Planning for the Future**

    Prepare for life's uncertainties with strategies for overcoming financial challenges and planning for long-term success.

10. **Financial Literacy for the Next Generation**

    Empower the next generation with the financial knowledge they need to thrive.

A Personal Journey

My name is Yong Deng Dau, and this book is deeply personal to me. Arriving in Australia from South Sudan at a young age, I faced the same uncertainties and challenges that many migrants experience. I had to learn how to navigate this new world, and through education, perseverance, and the support of others, I was able to build a future here. Today, I work in Banking and Financial Services, and my experiences have fueled a passion for helping others succeed.

The stories in this book—like those of Deng, John, and Ava—reflect the resilience and strength of the African migrant community in Australia. Deng's journey from South Sudan to building a thriving business, John's struggle to rebuild his financial life after moving from Kenya, and Ava's determination to secure a prosperous retirement after relocating from Rwanda—all of these stories highlight the challenges and triumphs that many of us share.

Each chapter is infused with the lessons we've learned, the challenges we've overcome, and the opportunities we've seized. My goal is to empower you with the knowledge and tools to create a future that reflects your dreams.

A Note on Financial Advice

While this book offers valuable insights and practical advice, it's important to remember that financial situations vary from person to person. The strategies presented here are based on general principles and may not suit everyone's unique circumstances. That's why I encourage you to consult with a qualified financial advisor who can tailor advice to your specific needs.

Moving Forward

The path to financial empowerment is not always easy, but it is always worth it. By applying the knowledge in this book, you are taking an essential step toward building a stable and prosperous future for yourself and your loved ones. Each chapter offers practical tools to help you overcome challenges, make informed decisions, and seize the opportunities that await you.

As you read, I encourage you to take action. Every small step you take brings you closer to financial freedom. You have the power to change your financial destiny, and this book is here to guide you along the way.

Thank you for choosing *From Ground Up: A Financial Empowerment for African Migrants in Australia.* May this guide be a beacon of hope, knowledge, and empowerment on your journey to financial success.

CHAPTER 1

UNDERSTANDING THE FINANCIAL SYSTEM IN AUSTRALIA

Introduction: John's Journey

John stood at the airport with his suitcase in hand, gazing out at the sprawling cityscape of Sydney, his new home. As an African migrant from Kenya, he was filled with a mix of excitement and uncertainty. The vibrant city, with its towering skyscrapers and bustling streets, was both awe-inspiring and intimidating. He marveled at the opportunities that lay ahead but was also aware of the challenges he would face in navigating a new financial landscape.

Back in Kenya, John had managed his finances within a familiar system, where he knew the rules and could easily access advice from family and friends. However, Australia presented a whole new world of financial norms, regulations, and institutions. Despite his strong financial background, John knew that understanding the intricacies of the Australian financial system would be crucial for securing a stable and prosperous future for himself and his family.

As he adjusted to his new surroundings, John encountered a variety of financial challenges that required him to adapt quickly. From understanding complex banking services to navigating tax regulations, each step was a learning experience. His journey was a testament to the importance of financial literacy and the need for a strategic approach to managing money in a new country.

1.1 The Structure of the Australian Financial System

John quickly realized that Australia's financial system was a sophisticated network of institutions, markets, and regulations, each playing a critical role in the country's economy. Understanding the basics was essential to making sense of this new environment.

1.1.1 Discovering Financial Institutions

John's first priority was to open a bank account. Armed with his passport, visa, and proof of address, he walked into a major bank branch. The banker, a friendly woman named Emily, greeted him warmly and began explaining the array of services available. Emily's explanations were thorough but complex, covering various types of accounts and financial products. John was familiar with savings accounts from his time in Kenya, but the array of options in Australia was overwhelming.

Emily patiently walked John through the different types of accounts:

- **Transaction Accounts:** These are the primary accounts for everyday banking needs, allowing for deposits, withdrawals, and bill payments. John was initially hesitant, concerned about fees and accessibility.

- **Credit Cards:** Emily explained that credit cards could be used for purchases and offered the advantage of building a credit history. John was intrigued but cautious, knowing the potential pitfalls of high-interest rates and debt accumulation.

- **Personal Loans:** These loans could be used for various purposes, from buying a car to funding personal projects. John was particularly interested in how these loans might support his goals of settling into his new home.

- **Investment Options:** Emily introduced John to the idea of investing, which was a new concept for him. She discussed various investment products, including term deposits and managed funds, which offered opportunities to grow his savings over time.

Initially, the range of services seemed overwhelming. However, as John asked questions and absorbed the information, the pieces began to fall into place. Emily reassured him that selecting the right bank account was just the beginning and that further advice would be available as he progressed.

John also learned about other types of financial institutions in Australia:

- **Credit Unions:** Smaller, member-owned institutions focused on community service. They might not have the extensive resources of major banks but often provide personalized service and lower fees. John appreciated the community-oriented approach of credit unions and considered them as an alternative for his banking needs.

- **Non-Bank Financial Institutions:** Including insurance companies and superannuation funds. These institutions don't offer everyday banking services but play crucial roles in managing risks and planning for retirement. John realized that understanding these institutions would be key to a well-rounded financial strategy.

Key Takeaways from John's Experience:

- Banks form the backbone of the financial system, providing a wide array of services essential for daily financial management.

- Credit unions offer a community-focused and often cost-effective alternative, which might align well with his values.

- Non-bank financial institutions are essential for managing insurance and retirement planning, adding another layer to his financial planning.

1.1.2 Learning About Financial Markets

As John settled into his new life, he began exploring ways to grow his money. Back in Kenya, he had heard about the stock market but lacked the opportunity to invest. Now, with a steady income, he was curious about the potential for investment.

John attended a financial literacy workshop at a local community centre. The workshop was led by Alex, a financial advisor who had a knack for breaking down complex topics into understandable segments. Alex discussed the Australian Securities Exchange (ASX) and how companies list their shares for public trading. John was fascinated by the concept of investing in companies and how this could lead to long-term wealth building.

John also discovered other financial markets in Australia:

- **Money Markets:** Where financial institutions trade short-term debt securities to manage liquidity. This market is more relevant to large institutions but is crucial for financial stability. Alex explained how money markets impact interest rates and overall economic stability, which John found intriguing but somewhat abstract.

- **Foreign Exchange Market:** Important for individuals like John who send money internationally. Understanding exchange rates and timing transfers can significantly affect the amount received by his family in Kenya. John was particularly interested in this aspect, as he needed to regularly send money back home. He learned about the factors affecting exchange rates and strategies to get the best value for his transfers.

Financial Market Overview

Market Type	Description	Relevance
Stock Market	Platform for buying and selling shares.	Opportunity for long-term investment.
Money Market	Short-term debt securities trading.	Essential for liquidity management of large institutions.
Foreign Exchange Market	Market for currency trading.	Important for international money transfers.

Key Takeaways from John's Experience:

- The stock market offers potential for long-term wealth but requires careful research and investment strategies.

- Money markets are vital for overall financial system stability, though less relevant to everyday consumers.

- Understanding exchange rates can optimize the value of international money transfers and ensure more effective financial support for his family.

1.1.3 Encountering Regulatory Bodies

One day, John noticed an unexpected increase in the interest rate on his loan. Confused and concerned, he delved into researching Australia's financial regulatory bodies. He wanted to understand who was responsible for regulating the financial system and how these institutions could impact his financial situation.

John discovered the following key regulatory bodies:

- **Reserve Bank of Australia (RBA):** Responsible for setting monetary policy and ensuring financial stability. John learned that the RBA's decisions on interest rates directly impact loans and savings. This was particularly relevant to him as he had recently taken out a loan and was curious about how interest rates could affect his repayments.

- **Australian Prudential Regulation Authority (APRA):** Oversees banks, credit unions, and insurance companies, ensuring their safe operation and protecting consumer interests. John found it reassuring to know that APRA worked to maintain the safety and soundness of financial institutions.

- **Australian Securities and Investments Commission (ASIC):** Regulates financial markets and protects consumers from unfair practices. ASIC handles disputes with financial institutions and ensures transparency in financial transactions. John appreciated ASIC's role in maintaining a fair financial environment.

- • **Australian Competition and Consumer Commission (ACCC):** Ensures fair treatment of consumers by businesses, including financial institutions. John realized the importance of the ACCC in promoting competition and protecting consumer rights.

Regulatory Body Overview

Regulatory Body	Role	Focus
Reserve Bank of Australia (RBA)	Sets monetary policy and maintains financial stability.	Interest rates, financial system stability.

Australian Prudential Regulation Authority (APRA)	Oversees financial institutions for safety and soundness.	Banks, credit unions, insurance companies.
Australian Securities and Investments Commission (ASIC)	Regulates financial markets and protects consumers.	Financial markets, consumer protection.
Australian Competition and Consumer Commission (ACCC)	Ensures fair treatment of consumers and promotes competition.	

Key Takeaways from John's Experience:

- The RBA, APRA, ASIC, and ACCC play crucial roles in maintaining the financial system's integrity and protecting consumer rights.

- Understanding these organizations helps in making informed decisions and resolving issues with financial institutions.

1.2 Understanding Financial Products and Services

John's journey extended beyond institutions and markets to the various financial products and services available to him. He realized that to effectively manage his finances, he needed to understand and select the right financial products.

1.2.1 Opening a Bank Account

John's first encounter with Australian financial products involved opening a transaction account. This type of account allowed him to manage everyday expenses like receiving his salary, paying bills, and making purchases.

He also learned about other types of accounts:

- **Savings Accounts:** Offered higher interest rates for money that isn't needed immediately. John saw this as a way to grow his savings with minimal risk. He chose to open a savings account to start building his emergency fund.

- **Term Deposits:** Required locking money away for a fixed period in exchange for higher interest rates. John was intrigued by term deposits as a way to earn more interest on his savings but was hesitant about the lack of liquidity.

John chose a basic transaction account and a savings account initially, planning to explore term deposits and other options as he became more comfortable with his financial situation. He realized that selecting the right type of account depended on his immediate needs and long-term financial goals.

Account Types Overview

Type of Account	Purpose	Features
Transaction Account	Daily expenses and transactions.	Debit card access, bill payments.
Savings Account	Saving money with higher interest.	Interest earnings, lower access.
Term Deposit	Fixed deposit for higher interest.	Fixed term, higher interest, less liquidity.

Key Takeaways from John's Experience:

- Different types of bank accounts serve various purposes, from everyday transactions to long-term savings.

- Understanding the features and limitations of each account type helps in choosing the right one for specific needs.

1.2.2 Exploring Credit Options

John's experience with credit cards was both exciting and daunting. He had heard about credit cards as a tool for convenience and building credit history but was wary of the potential for high-interest rates and debt.

Emily explained the concept of credit cards and their benefits:

- **Building Credit History:** Responsible use of credit cards can help build a positive credit history, which is important for future loans and financial transactions. John learned that a good credit history could open doors to better financial opportunities.

- **Rewards and Benefits:** Many credit cards offer rewards programs, cashback, and other perks. John was interested in these benefits but needed to weigh them against the potential costs and interest rates.

John decided to apply for a credit card with a low annual fee and manageable interest rate. He committed to using it responsibly, paying off the balance in full each month to avoid interest charges. He also set reminders to track his spending and avoid exceeding his budget.

Credit Card Considerations

- **Interest Rates:** Higher rates can lead to significant debt if balances are not paid off in full. John carefully selected a card with a reasonable interest rate.

- **Fees and Charges:** Look for annual fees, foreign transaction fees, and other costs. John chose a card with minimal fees to keep costs down.

Key Takeaways from John's Experience:

- Credit cards can offer benefits but require careful management to avoid debt and high-interest charges.

- Building a positive credit history through responsible use is crucial for future financial success.

1.2.3 Planning for Retirement with Superannuation

John's employer automatically enrolled him in a superannuation fund, which was a new concept for him. In Kenya, retirement planning was less formalized, so the Australian superannuation system required a significant adjustment.

John took the time to understand superannuation and its implications for his retirement:

- **Accumulation Funds:** He learned that these funds grow over time through contributions and investment returns. John realized the importance of reviewing the performance and fees associated with his fund to maximize growth.

- **Self-Managed Superannuation Funds (SMSFs):** John explored SMSFs as an option for more control over his retirement savings. Although SMSFs offered flexibility, they also required a higher level of management and compliance.

John compared different superannuation options, considering factors such as fees, investment choices, and historical performance. He chose a superannuation fund that aligned with his risk tolerance and retirement goals.

Superannuation Options Overview

Option	Description	Consideration
Accumulation Fund	Contributions and returns grow over time	Fees, investment options, performance.
Self-Managed Superannuation Fund (SMSF)	Personal control over superannuation investments.	Greater responsibility, compliance.

Key Takeaways from John's Experience:

- Understanding superannuation and selecting the right fund is crucial for effective retirement planning.

- Exploring different superannuation options helps in making informed decisions for long-term financial security.

1.3 Managing Your Finances: Practical Tips

As John continued his journey, he realized that practical financial management was key to achieving his goals. He implemented several strategies to stay on track with his finances.

1.3.1 Creating a Budget

John's first step in managing his finances was to create a budget. He categorized his expenses into essential and non-essential items. This approach helped him prioritize his spending and allocate funds for savings.

John used a budgeting app to track his expenses and set spending limits. He found that budgeting apps were effective in providing insights into his spending patterns and helping him stay within his budget.

John adopted the 50/30/20 rule as a guideline:

- **50% for Needs:** Allocated to essential expenses like housing, utilities, and groceries.

- **30% for Wants:** Budgeted for non-essential items like dining out, entertainment, and travel.

- **20% for Savings and Debt Repayment:** Dedicated to building savings and repaying debt.

Budgeting Tools

- **Mobile Apps:** Apps like Mint, YNAB, and PocketGuard offer easy tracking of expenses and budgeting insights.

- **Spreadsheets:** Customized spreadsheets allow for detailed tracking and budgeting tailored to individual needs.

Key Takeaways from John's Experience:

- Budgeting helps manage expenses effectively and prioritize savings and investments.

- Utilizing budgeting tools and apps simplifies the process and provides valuable insights into spending habits.

1.3.2 Building an Emergency Fund

John understood the importance of having an emergency fund. He set aside a portion of his income into a high-yield savings account specifically for emergencies. This fund provided him with peace of mind and financial security in case of unexpected events.

John's goal was to accumulate three to six months' worth of living expenses in his emergency fund. He chose a high-yield savings account to earn interest while keeping the funds accessible.

Emergency Fund Considerations

- **Liquidity:** The fund should be easily accessible in case of emergencies, so a high-yield savings account or money market account is ideal.

- **Amount:** Aim for three to six months of living expenses, depending on personal circumstances and job stability.

Key Takeaways from John's Experience:

- An emergency fund provides financial security and reduces the risk of falling into debt during unforeseen circumstances.

- Setting a target amount and consistently contributing to the fund can ensure its effectiveness.

1.3.3 Understanding Taxation

John's experience with taxation in Australia was another area of learning. He needed to understand income tax, GST, and other relevant taxes.

John learned that Australia has a progressive tax system, where higher incomes are taxed at higher rates. He reviewed his income tax obligations and explored ways to claim eligible deductions, such as work-related expenses and charitable donations. Consulting with a tax professional helped him navigate the complexities of tax filing and ensure compliance.

Tax Types Overview

Type of Tax	Description	Considerations
Income Tax	Tax on earnings from employment or other sources.	Progressive rates, deductions, tax returns.
Goods and Services Tax (GST)	Tax on goods and services purchased.	Usually included in the price of items.

Key Takeaways from John's Experience:
- Understanding the tax system helps manage obligations and optimize tax benefits.

- Seeking professional advice ensures compliance and effective tax planning.

1.4 Navigating Financial Challenges

John faced several financial challenges as he adjusted to his new life in Australia. Here's how he approached and overcame these challenges:

1.4.1 Dealing with Debt

John initially struggled with managing debt from his car loan and other expenses. He realized the importance of addressing high-interest debt first and developed a debt repayment plan.

John prioritized paying off credit card balances and personal loans while maintaining minimum payments on other debts. He explored options for consolidating his debt, which could potentially lower interest rates and simplify payments.

John also focused on maintaining a good credit score, which was essential for future borrowing and financial opportunities. He created a detailed debt repayment schedule and committed to it, which helped him achieve financial stability.

Debt Management Strategies
- **Debt Snowball Method:** Focus on paying off the smallest debt first while making minimum payments on larger debts. Once the smallest debt is paid off, move to the next smallest debt.

- **Debt Avalanche Method:** Focus on paying off the debt with the highest interest rate first to save on interest payments over time.

Key Takeaways from John's Experience:

- Prioritizing high-interest debt and developing a repayment plan can alleviate financial stress.

- Consolidating debt and managing credit responsibly can improve financial stability and future borrowing conditions.

1.4.2 Planning for Major Expenses

John began planning for major expenses, such as home renovations and future vacations. He set specific savings goals for these expenses and allocated a portion of his monthly budget to achieve them.

John explored options for financing major expenses, including using savings or taking out a low-interest loan. He found that careful planning and saving in advance prevented financial strain and allowed him to afford desired purchases without falling into debt.

Major Expense Planning Tips

- **Set Clear Goals:** Define specific amounts and timelines for major expenses.

- **Save Regularly:** Allocate a portion of income to savings for planned expenses.

- **Evaluate Financing Options:** Compare interest rates and terms for loans or other financing methods.

Key Takeaways from John's Experience:

- Planning and saving for major expenses helps avoid financial strain and ensures affordability.

- Exploring financing options and setting clear savings goals can facilitate better financial management.

Conclusion: Embracing Financial Literacy

John's journey through Australia's financial system was both challenging and rewarding. His efforts to understand the financial landscape, manage his finances wisely, and navigate challenges were instrumental in building a solid financial foundation.

John's experience highlights the importance of financial literacy for African migrants and anyone navigating a new financial environment. Embracing financial education, seeking advice when needed, and staying informed about financial matters can lead to better financial decisions and long-term success.

As John looked back on his journey, he felt a deep sense of accomplishment. He had transformed from a newcomer overwhelmed by financial complexities to a confident individual managing his finances effectively. His story serves as an inspiration for others embarking on similar journeys, emphasizing that with patience, persistence, and the right knowledge, financial success is within reach.

Additional Resources

To further assist readers in their financial journey, John found the following resources invaluable:

- **Financial Literacy Workshops:** Local community centers and online platforms often offer workshops on budgeting, investing, and other financial topics.

- **Financial Advisors:** Consulting with a certified financial advisor can provide personalized guidance and help with complex financial decisions.

- **Online Financial Tools:** Websites and apps offer tools for budgeting, investing, and tracking expenses, making financial management more accessible.

By utilizing these resources and continuing to seek knowledge, individuals can navigate their financial journeys with confidence and achieve their financial goals.

CHAPTER 2

BUDGETING AND FINANCIAL PLANNING (DENG'S JOURNEY)

Introduction: Deng's New Beginnings

Deng stepped off the plane in Melbourne, feeling the cool breeze of the Australian winter against his skin. It was his first time outside South Sudan, and everything felt new and overwhelming. Australia promised a fresh start—a place where Deng could build a life for himself, free from the instability and conflict that had marked his past.

As he settled into his new life, Deng found himself grappling with a mix of excitement and anxiety. The streets of Melbourne were a far cry from the dusty roads of his hometown in South Sudan. Everything seemed faster, louder, and more expensive. Deng was determined to succeed, but he quickly realized that achieving his dreams in Australia would require more than just hard work—it would require careful financial planning.

Deng came from a large family, and as the eldest son, he felt a deep sense of responsibility to support his parents and siblings back home. Managing his finances became crucial, not just for himself but for his family as well. With this in mind, Deng began his journey to financial independence, eager to learn how to budget, save, and invest wisely.

2.1 The Importance of Budgeting: Learning the Basics

In his first few weeks in Melbourne, Deng focused on settling into his new routine. He had found a small apartment in the western suburbs, started a job at a logistics company, and began attending English classes in the evenings. But as the weeks went by, Deng started to feel the weight of his financial responsibilities. His rent was higher than expected, and his paychecks didn't stretch as far as he had hoped.

One day, after receiving a particularly large electricity bill, Deng decided that he needed to take control of his finances. He had heard about budgeting from a friend back home, but he had never really practiced it. Now, it seemed like a necessity. Deng sat down at his small kitchen table with a notebook and pen, determined to figure out how to manage his money effectively.

2.1.1 Why Budgeting Matters: Deng's Epiphany

As Deng began jotting down his income and expenses, he realized why budgeting was so important. He had been living from paycheck to paycheck, without a clear plan for his money. That had to change.

1. **Control Over Finances:**
   Before budgeting, Deng felt like his money was slipping through his fingers. Each month, he would receive his paycheck, pay a few bills, and suddenly find himself short on cash. By creating a budget, Deng gained control over his finances. He could allocate his income effectively, ensuring that essential expenses were covered and that he saved for future needs.

2. **Goal Achievement:**
   Deng had big dreams. He wanted to save enough money to bring his younger sister, Aluel, to Australia. He also hoped to buy a car, travel around the country, and one day own a home. By tracking his

spending and setting savings targets, Deng realized that a budget could help him work toward these goals. It was the key to turning his dreams into reality.

3. **Financial Awareness:**

   Budgeting also increased Deng's awareness of where his money was going. Before creating a budget, he hadn't realized how much he was spending on things like dining out or entertainment subscriptions. By becoming more aware of his spending habits, Deng could identify areas where he could cut back and reallocate funds to better align with his priorities.

One evening, Deng spoke to a friend from his English class about budgeting. His friend, Samuel, had been living in Australia for several years and had successfully built a savings cushion. Samuel explained how budgeting had helped him stay on track and avoid unnecessary stress. Inspired by this conversation, Deng felt even more motivated to take control of his finances.

2.1.2 How to Create a Budget: Deng's First Steps

With his newfound understanding of budgeting, Deng decided to create a more detailed plan. He followed these steps:

1. **Assessing Income**

   Deng's primary source of income was his job at the logistics company. His monthly salary was enough to cover his basic living expenses, but not much more. Deng also did occasional freelance work, helping friends and neighbors with small repairs and renovations. He made sure to account for all of his income, including these side gigs, so he had a complete picture of his earnings.

2. **Identifying Expenses**

   Next, Deng listed all of his expenses. He started with the fixed costs—rent, utilities, and transportation. These were non-negotiable expenses that he had to pay every month. Then, Deng moved on to variable costs, like groceries, entertainment, and dining out. These expenses fluctuated from month to month, but Deng knew he needed to keep track of them to stay within his budget.

As he listed his expenses, Deng noticed that some of his spending habits were more indulgent than necessary. He had been eating out more than he should, and his subscription services were adding up. Deng realized that cutting back on these expenses could help him save more money for his long-term goals.

Deng also realized that sending money back to his family in South Sudan was a priority for him. Each month, he set aside a portion of his income to send to his parents and siblings. This was a non-negotiable part of his budget, and Deng was proud to be able to support his family, even from thousands of kilometers away.

3. **Calculating the Budget**

After listing his income and expenses, Deng subtracted his total expenses from his total income to see where he stood. Thankfully, he had a small surplus, but it wasn't much. Deng decided to allocate this extra money toward his savings, making sure he was setting aside funds for his future.

4. **Monitoring and Adjusting**

Deng knew that life was unpredictable, and his financial situation could change at any moment. That's why he committed to reviewing his budget regularly. Every month, Deng would sit down and track his spending, making adjustments as needed. If he received a bonus at work or had an unexpected expense, Deng would update his budget to reflect these changes. This practice helped him stay on top of his finances and ensure that he was always moving toward his goals.

2.2 Financial Planning Basics: Mapping Out the Future

Once Deng had a solid budget in place, he began to think about the bigger picture. Budgeting was a great start, but Deng knew that if he wanted to achieve his long-term goals, he needed a comprehensive financial plan.

Financial planning involved more than just tracking his income and expenses. It required setting clear goals, saving for the future, investing wisely, and managing risks. Deng realized that a well-developed financial plan would help him make informed decisions and prepare for unexpected events.

One Saturday afternoon, Deng sat down with Samuel, his friend from English class, to discuss financial planning. Samuel had been working with a financial adviser for several years and had built a robust financial plan. Over coffee, Samuel shared his experiences with Deng, explaining how setting financial goals and creating a plan had helped him achieve stability and peace of mind.

2.2.1 Setting Financial Goals: Dreaming Big

Deng was inspired by Samuel's story and decided it was time to write down his own financial goals—big and small. He had always been a dreamer, but now, in this new chapter of his life, Deng wanted to turn those dreams into concrete plans.

He divided his goals into three categories:

1. **Short-Term Goals**

    Deng's short-term goals were things he wanted to achieve within the next year. At the top of the list was saving for a plane ticket for his sister, Aluel. He also wanted to pay off his credit card debt, which had accumulated during his first few months in Australia. Finally, Deng set a goal to build an emergency fund—a safety net for unexpected expenses.

2. **Medium-Term Goals**

   Deng's medium-term goals spanned one to five years. He hoped to buy a car within the next couple of years, which would make his daily commute much easier. He also wanted to take a trip back to South Sudan to visit his family and show them how far he had come. Additionally, Deng started thinking about taking some courses to further his education and improve his job prospects.

3. **Long-Term Goals**

   Deng's long-term goals were the big dreams—the ones that would take years of hard work and dedication to achieve. First on the list was buying a home. Deng had always dreamed of owning his own place, and he was determined to make that dream a reality. He also began thinking about retirement, even though it seemed far off. Deng knew that the earlier he started saving for retirement, the better off he would be in the future.

   With his goals clearly outlined, Deng felt more motivated than ever. He knew that by taking small, consistent steps, he could achieve anything he set his mind to.

2.2.2 Developing a Financial Plan: A Step-by-Step Approach

Now that Deng had his goals in place, he needed a plan to achieve them. He broke down his financial plan into several key components:

1. **Budgeting and Saving**

   Deng incorporated his budget into his financial plan, ensuring that he was setting aside money each month for savings. He opened a separate savings account specifically for his emergency fund, making sure that this money was easily accessible in case of an emergency. Deng also set up automatic transfers to his savings account, ensuring he would stay on track without having to think about it every month.

Deng's decision to open multiple savings accounts for different purposes helped him stay organized.

Deng's decision to open multiple savings accounts for different purposes helped him stay organized. One account was dedicated to his emergency fund, while another was reserved for short-term goals like his sister's plane ticket. Having separate accounts allowed Deng to keep his financial priorities clear and prevented him from dipping into funds that were meant for specific goals.

2. **Investment Planning**

Deng knew that saving money was important, but he also wanted to grow his wealth over time. He began researching investment options, such as stocks, bonds, and mutual funds. Deng learned that investing could be a powerful tool for building wealth, but it also came with risks. To manage these risks, Deng decided to diversify his investments.

He didn't jump into the stock market without preparation. Deng started by educating himself. He attended financial workshops offered by community organizations and took online courses on basic investing principles. These efforts helped him understand how to evaluate different types of investments and make informed decisions.

Deng eventually opened an investment account with a small portion of his savings. He chose low-risk mutual funds to start with, knowing that this was a safer way to ease into the world of investing. As his confidence grew, Deng planned to diversify further by including stocks and real estate in his portfolio. His ultimate goal was to build a balanced portfolio that could generate returns without exposing him to excessive risk.

3. **Risk Management**

Deng understood that life was unpredictable, and financial security required planning for the unexpected. He began thinking about how he could protect himself from unforeseen challenges. After talking to some of his colleagues, Deng realized that insurance was a critical part of risk management.

Health insurance was Deng's first priority. Although Australia had a public healthcare system, Deng opted to supplement it with private health insurance for additional coverage. He also considered other types of insurance, such as life insurance and car insurance, to protect his growing assets. Though he didn't yet own a car, he planned ahead, knowing that he would need coverage when he purchased one.

Deng's approach to insurance wasn't just about protecting himself—it was also about safeguarding his family. He wanted to make sure that if anything happened to him, his loved ones wouldn't be burdened with financial difficulties. This sense of responsibility guided his decisions and motivated him to plan for every eventuality.

4. **Retirement Planning**

Retirement seemed like a distant goal, but Deng knew that it was never too early to start planning for it. He had learned about the Australian superannuation system, where employers contribute a portion of their employees' salaries to a retirement fund. Deng decided to contribute additional money to his superannuation fund whenever possible, even if it meant sacrificing some of his short-term luxuries.

5. **Deng began learning about other retirement savings options, like personal super contributions and investment accounts designed for retirement. He knew that by starting early and being consistent, he could build a comfortable retirement fund that would support him in his later years. Planning for retirement also gave Deng peace of mind, knowing that he was taking steps to secure his future.**

6. **Estate Planning**

Although Deng was still young, he understood the importance of preparing for the future. He didn't have much in the way of assets yet, but he knew that creating a will and thinking about estate planning would be essential as he built wealth. Deng began researching the basics of estate planning, learning about the legal processes involved in distributing assets after death. Though it wasn't a pleasant topic to think about, Deng felt more secure knowing that his family would be taken care of if anything ever happened to him.

2.3 Managing Debt: Facing Financial Challenges

Deng had made significant progress in managing his finances, but he knew that one of his biggest obstacles was dealing with debt. Like many newcomers, Deng had relied on credit cards to cover some of his initial expenses in Australia. While the credit had been helpful in the beginning, Deng was now determined to pay off his balances and avoid the pitfalls of debt.

2.3.1 Types of Debt: Understanding the Burden

As Deng educated himself about personal finance, he began to understand the different types of debt he was dealing with:

1. **Revolving Debt**

Deng's credit card debt was a form of revolving debt, which allowed him to borrow up to a certain limit and carry a balance from month to month. However, Deng quickly realized that the interest rates on his credit cards were high, making it difficult to pay off the balance if he only made the minimum payments. He knew that he needed a strategy to tackle this debt head-on.

2. **Installment Debt**

   Deng also had a car loan, which was an installment debt. Unlike his credit card, the car loan had a fixed repayment schedule with set monthly payments. The interest rate on the loan was lower than his credit card, and Deng appreciated the predictability of the payments. Still, he was eager to pay off the loan early if possible, freeing up more of his income for savings and investments.

3. **Secured Debt**

   The car loan was also an example of secured debt, meaning it was backed by collateral—in this case, the car itself. Deng understood that if he defaulted on his payments, the lender could repossess the vehicle. This added pressure made Deng more determined to stay on top of his loan payments and avoid falling behind.

4. **Unsecured Debt**

   Unlike his car loan, Deng's credit card was unsecured debt, meaning there was no collateral backing it. Because of this, the interest rates were higher, and missing payments could hurt his credit score. Deng realized that tackling his credit card debt was a top priority if he wanted to avoid long-term financial damage.

2.3.2 Strategies for Managing Debt: Deng's Game Plan

With a clear understanding of his debt, Deng began developing strategies to pay it off and regain his financial freedom:

1. **Prioritize Payments**

   Deng knew that the key to managing debt was to prioritize his payments. He decided to focus on paying off his high-interest credit card debt first. By making larger payments on his credit card, Deng could reduce the balance more quickly and save money on interest.

Once his credit card was paid off, Deng would shift his focus to his car loan, aiming to pay it off early.

2. **Consolidate Debt**

   Deng considered consolidating his debts into a single loan with a lower interest rate. Debt consolidation could simplify his payments and potentially reduce the overall interest he would pay. However, Deng was cautious about taking on more debt, so he researched his options carefully before making a decision.

3. **Negotiate with Creditors**

   Deng wasn't afraid to advocate for himself. When he found himself struggling with a particularly high-interest rate on one of his credit cards, Deng contacted the credit card company to negotiate a lower rate. To his surprise, the company was willing to work with him, reducing the interest rate and making it easier for Deng to manage his payments. This experience taught Deng the importance of communication and persistence when dealing with creditors.

4. **Avoid New Debt**

   While managing his existing debt, Deng made a conscious effort to avoid taking on new debt. He stopped using his credit cards for everyday purchases, opting to use cash or debit instead. This approach helped Deng stay within his budget and avoid the temptation of spending money he didn't have.

2.4 Saving for the Future: Building a Safety Net

With his debt management plan in place, Deng turned his attention to saving for the future. He understood that financial stability wasn't just about paying off debt—it was also about building a safety net and preparing for long-term goals.

2.4.1   Emergency Fund: A Cushion for the Unexpected

Deng's first priority was to build an emergency fund. He had heard horror stories from friends who had faced unexpected expenses—medical bills, car repairs, or sudden job loss—with no savings to fall back on. Deng didn't want to be in that position, so he committed to setting aside a portion of his income each month for emergencies.

He set a goal to save three to six months' worth of living expenses in a readily accessible account. This emergency fund would be his financial cushion, giving him peace of mind knowing that he could handle whatever life threw at him.

2.4.2   Retirement Savings: Planning for the Long Haul

Retirement still seemed like a distant dream, but Deng knew that the earlier he started saving, the better off he would be. He continued contributing to his superannuation fund, ensuring that his retirement savings grew steadily over time.

Deng also began exploring additional retirement savings options. He considered making personal contributions to his superannuation fund, which would allow him to boost his savings even further. He also looked into investment accounts designed specifically for retirement, weighing the pros and cons of each option. By taking these steps, Deng was laying the groundwork for a comfortable and secure retirement, even though it was still years away.

2.4.3   Investment Savings: Growing Wealth Over Time

Deng wasn't content with just saving money—he wanted to grow his wealth over time. That's when he began exploring investment options. Deng learned that investing could be a powerful tool for building wealth, but it required careful planning and a willingness to take on some risk.

He started small, investing in a few low-risk mutual funds and bonds. As he grew more comfortable with investing, Deng began diversifying his portfolio, adding stocks and real estate investments into the mix. By spreading his investments across different asset classes, Deng was able to reduce risk while maximizing his potential returns.

Deng also made a point to educate himself about the stock market and different investment strategies. He read books, attended financial workshops, and even joined an online investment community where he could learn from others who were more experienced in the field. These efforts paid off, as Deng began to see his investments grow steadily over time. Each month, Deng reviewed his investment portfolio to ensure it aligned with his long-term goals. He learned that investing wasn't just about making quick gains—it was about patience and strategic decision-making. Slowly but surely, his investments started to yield returns, contributing to his overall financial security.

By staying disciplined with his budget, managing his debt, and making wise investments, Deng was building a future where his dreams of owning a home, helping his family, and enjoying a comfortable retirement were within reach. Every small step he took brought him closer to the life he envisioned when he first stepped off the plane in Melbourne.

2.5 Conclusion: Deng's Financial Transformation

As Deng reflected on his journey, he realized just how far he had come. When he first arrived in Australia, Deng had felt overwhelmed by the complexities of managing his finances in a new country. But through dedication, learning, and careful planning, he had transformed his financial situation.

Deng now had a solid budget in place, guiding him each month and helping him stay on track with his expenses and savings. He had developed a comprehensive financial plan that included everything from budgeting and saving to investing and retirement planning. By setting clear goals, Deng was able to take concrete steps toward achieving his dreams, whether it was paying off debt, bringing his sister to Australia, or one day owning his own home.

Debt, once a daunting burden, was now something Deng managed with confidence. He had paid off a significant portion of his credit card debt and was well on his way to clearing the rest. His car loan was manageable, and Deng knew that with continued focus and discipline, he could pay it off early.

Beyond debt management, Deng had built a safety net for himself in the form of an emergency fund. He no longer feared unexpected expenses, knowing that he had a financial cushion to fall back on if needed. And with his retirement savings steadily growing, Deng felt secure in the knowledge that he was planning for a comfortable future.

Investing had also become a key part of Deng's financial strategy. What once seemed like an intimidating and complex world was now an opportunity for Deng to grow his wealth and work toward his long-term financial goals. Through education and careful decision-making, Deng had built a diversified investment portfolio that balanced risk and reward, ensuring steady growth over time.

2.6 Moving Forward: Continuing the Journey

Deng knew that his financial journey was far from over. In fact, he saw it as a lifelong process—one that required continuous learning, adaptation, and commitment. As he looked to the future, Deng felt optimistic about the opportunities ahead. He was determined to continue building on the foundation he had created, refining his financial plan, and achieving his goals one step at a time.

He reminded himself that financial success wasn't about perfection. There would be setbacks along the way—unexpected expenses, market fluctuations, and life events that could throw him off course. But Deng had learned that resilience and persistence were key. By staying focused on his long-term goals and adapting his strategies as needed, Deng knew that he could overcome any challenges that came his way.

Deng's journey was also a reminder of the importance of community. He had relied on the support of friends, mentors, and professionals to guide him through the complexities of personal finance. Whether it was advice from a financial adviser, tips from a colleague, or simply sharing his experiences with others, Deng had benefited from the knowledge and support of those around him. Moving forward, Deng was committed to helping others in his community navigate their own financial journeys, sharing what he had learned and offering support whenever he could.

As Deng continued his journey, he carried with him a sense of pride and accomplishment. He had taken control of his finances, built a solid foundation for the future, and empowered himself to achieve his dreams. And for Deng, that was just the beginning.

FAQs: Learning from Deng's Journey

Q1: What is the best way to start budgeting if I have never done it before?

A1: Start by tracking your income and expenses to understand your spending patterns. Use budgeting tools or apps to create a budget that allocates funds for essential expenses, savings, and discretionary spending.

Review and adjust your budget regularly to stay on track with your financial goals.

Q2: How can I set realistic financial goals?

A2: Set SMART goals that are specific, measurable, attainable, relevant, and time-bound. Break larger goals into smaller, manageable steps, and create a plan to achieve them. Reflect on your priorities and consider both short-term and long-term objectives.

Q3: What should I do if I am struggling with debt?

A3: Prioritize paying off high-interest debt first and consider consolidating or negotiating with creditors. Focus on cutting unnecessary expenses and seek professional advice if needed to create a debt management plan. Avoid taking on new debt while managing your existing balances.

Q4: How much should I save in an emergency fund?

A4: Aim to save three to six months' worth of living expenses in an emergency fund. This amount provides a financial cushion for unexpected expenses or emergencies. Keep your emergency fund in an easily accessible account so you can access it quickly if needed.

Q5: What types of investments should I consider for long-term growth?

A5: Consider a diversified portfolio of investments, including stocks, bonds, mutual funds, and real estate. Your investment choices should align with your risk tolerance and financial goals. Consult a financial adviser for personalized advice and ensure that your investment strategy is regularly reviewed and adjusted as needed.

By following Deng's story, readers can learn valuable lessons about budgeting, financial planning, debt management, and saving for the future. Deng's journey is a testament to the power of discipline, education, and perseverance in achieving financial stability and success.

CHAPTER 3

UNDERSTANDING CREDIT AND LOANS (ADHIEU'S JOURNEY)

Introduction: Adhieu's First Encounter with Credit

Adhieu, a South Sudanese woman in her late twenties, stood at the counter of a bank in Sydney, Australia, feeling a mixture of excitement and apprehension. It had been just over a year since she arrived in Australia, and she was adjusting to the new culture, opportunities, and challenges. One of the most significant challenges she faced was understanding the concept of credit. Back in South Sudan, her financial life was straightforward—she dealt only in cash. There were no credit cards, no loans, no credit scores. Everything was tangible and immediate. But in Australia, credit seemed to be everywhere. From the advertisements on television to the conversations she overheard at work, credit was a key part of the financial landscape.

One afternoon, after her shift at the local healthcare facility, her colleague, Sophie, casually mentioned the benefits of having a credit card. "It's great for building your credit score," Sophie said. "And it can really help in emergencies."

Adhieu nodded, but deep down, she had no idea how credit worked. The concept of borrowing money and paying it back over time was foreign to her. Sophie could sense her hesitation and offered to accompany her to the bank to explain the process. And that's how Adhieu found herself at the bank, ready to apply for her first credit card—a moment that would mark the beginning of her financial journey in Australia.

With Sophie's guidance, Adhieu took her first steps into the world of credit. It wasn't just about survival in a new country anymore; it was about thriving. Understanding and using credit wisely became essential not only for her success but also for her ultimate goal: building a secure future for herself and her family.

3.1 Fundamentals of Credit: A New World

As Adhieu sat with the bank advisor, she began to grasp the basics of credit. The advisor explained that credit was essentially borrowed money that had to be repaid, often with interest. Unlike South Sudan, where financial transactions were straightforward and cash-based, Australia's financial system relied heavily on credit. Here, people used credit for everyday purchases, from groceries to cars, and even homes. This realization was both intriguing and intimidating to Adhieu. In her home country, debt was something to be avoided at all costs. Now, she was learning that in Australia, credit could be a valuable tool—if managed carefully.

The bank advisor also introduced her to the concept of a credit score, a number that reflected her creditworthiness based on her credit history. This score would determine her ability to borrow money, secure loans, and even influence her ability to rent an apartment or get a job. Adhieu realized that building and maintaining a good credit score would be crucial to achieving her financial goals in Australia.

Cultural Reflection:

Back in South Sudan, money was often a communal affair. Family members helped each other out, and debts were settled through mutual understanding. In Australia, everything felt more individualistic—credit scores were personal, and financial mistakes could follow you for years. This difference in approach often weighed on Adhieu's mind. She found herself reconciling her desire to support her family back home with the need to build her own financial future in Australia.

3.1.1 Types of Credit: Exploring the Options

The bank advisor walked Adhieu through the different types of credit available in Australia, each serving a unique purpose:

1. **Revolving Credit**

   Revolving credit worked like a revolving door—it allowed you to borrow up to a certain limit, repay, and borrow again. A credit card was the most common form of revolving credit. The advisor explained that with a credit card, Adhieu could make purchases and then pay off the balance over time. However, she needed to be careful with interest rates if she didn't pay the full amount each month.

   Sophie had warned her about the risks of revolving credit. "It's easy to swipe that card and forget about the consequences," Sophie said. "But if you don't pay it off in full, the interest can pile up quickly."

   "It's just so different from how we did things back home," Adhieu admitted. "In South Sudan, if you didn't have the money, you didn't spend it. Here, it feels like everyone lives on borrowed money."

   "That's true," Sophie said thoughtfully. "But the trick is to use it wisely. Build your credit, but don't rely on it too much. It's about balance."

2. **Installment Credit**

   Installment credit, on the other hand, was more straightforward. This type of credit involved borrowing a specific amount of money, like for a car loan or personal loan, and repaying it in fixed monthly installments over a set period. The advisor explained that installment loans often came with lower interest rates than credit cards, making them a more affordable option for larger purchases.

Adhieu thought about the possibilities. Maybe one day, she would need an installment loan to buy a car or even a home. But for now, she was content with understanding the basics.

3. **Open Credit**

Open credit was a new concept for Adhieu. The bank advisor explained that open credit required paying off the full balance by the due date each month, without carrying it over. Utilities and some retail accounts were examples of this. There was no interest charged if the balance was paid on time, but missing a payment could result in penalties. This was similar to the way bills were handled back in South Sudan, but with the added complication of credit history and potential penalties.

3.1.2 Credit Scores: The Key to Financial Health

As the conversation continued, the bank advisor introduced another key concept: the credit score. This three-digit number, ranging from 300 to 850, was a reflection of her creditworthiness. The advisor explained that lenders would use this score to determine how much of a risk it would be to lend her money. The higher the score, the better the terms she could get on loans and credit cards.

1. **Definition**

A credit score is a numerical representation of an individual's creditworthiness based on their credit history. It reflects their ability to manage debt and make timely payments. For Adhieu, this was a completely new idea. In South Sudan, financial reliability was based on reputation within the community. Here, it was a number generated by financial institutions.

2. **Factors Affecting Credit Scores**

Several factors influence a credit score, the advisor explained:

◎ **Payment history:** Whether she paid her bills on time.

- ◎ **Credit utilization:** How much of her available credit she was using.

- ◎ **Length of credit history:** How long she had been using credit.

- ◎ **Types of credit accounts:** Whether she had a mix of credit types, like revolving and installment credit.

- ◎ **Recent credit inquiries:** Whether she had applied for new credit recently.

3. **Each of these factors contributed to her overall score, and by managing them carefully, she could improve her creditworthiness over time.**

4. **Credit Score Ranges**

   The bank advisor showed her a chart that broke down credit scores into ranges. Scores typically ranged from 300 to 850. A score above 700 was considered good, while anything below 600 might make it harder to get approved for loans or favorable interest rates. This information was eye-opening for Adhieu. She realized that maintaining a good credit score would be essential for her future in Australia, especially if she ever wanted to buy a home or start a business.

3.2 Managing and Improving Credit: A Journey of Responsibility

Armed with this new knowledge, Adhieu was determined to manage her credit responsibly. She understood that building a strong credit profile would take time and effort, but she was committed to the process. After all, her financial future—and the future of her family—depended on it.

As she walked out of the bank with her new credit card in hand, she felt a sense of empowerment. This was a tool that could help her achieve her dreams, as long as she used it wisely.

3.2.1 Building Good Credit: Laying the Foundation

The first step in managing credit was to build a solid foundation. Adhieu knew that she needed to establish good habits from the start.

1. **Pay Bills on Time**

   One of the most important factors in building good credit was paying bills on time. Adhieu set up reminders on her phone to ensure that she never missed a payment, whether it was for her credit card, utility bills, or rent. She knew that late payments could hurt her credit score, and she was determined to avoid that at all costs.

   She remembered the struggles of her family back in South Sudan, where even the smallest financial misstep could have long-lasting consequences. Here, in Australia, she had more control over her financial future, and she wasn't going to let that slip away.

2. **Maintain Low Credit Utilization**

   Another important factor was credit utilization—the percentage of her available credit that she was using. The bank advisor had advised her to keep this ratio below 30%, meaning that if her credit limit was $1,000, she should try not to spend more than $300 at any given time. By keeping her credit utilization low, she could maintain a healthy credit score and avoid the pitfalls of revolving debt.

   This was a concept that took some getting used to. In South Sudan, if you had money, you spent it. If you didn't, you didn't spend. Here, the idea of having access to money that wasn't really yours was both tempting and dangerous. But with discipline, she knew she could manage it but with discipline, she knew she could manage it. This mindset of caution and responsibility became her guiding principle. She would remind herself often that just because she had access to credit didn't mean she should use it recklessly.

3. **Diversify Credit Accounts**

Over time, Adhieu learned that diversifying her credit accounts could strengthen her credit profile. For now, she had her credit card, but she was open to the idea of taking out a small personal loan in the future, perhaps to invest in a business venture or further her education. The bank advisor had explained that having a mix of credit types—such as revolving credit from her credit card and installment credit from a loan—could positively impact her credit score, as long as she managed them responsibly.

However, she knew that diversifying her credit was a step she would only take when she felt ready. Her focus at this stage was on mastering the basics—making timely payments, keeping her balances low, and monitoring her credit closely.

3.2.2 Monitoring Credit: Staying Vigilant

Managing credit wasn't just about making timely payments—it was also about staying informed. Adhieu knew that monitoring her credit was essential to avoiding any potential pitfalls, such as errors on her credit report or signs of identity theft.

1. **Check Your Credit Report Regularly**

The bank advisor recommended that she check her credit report at least once a year. In Australia, she could request a free credit report from major credit reporting agencies like Equifax, Experian, and illion. This was an opportunity to ensure that all the information on her report was accurate and that there were no discrepancies that could negatively impact her credit score.

The first time she checked her credit report, Adhieu was nervous. The idea of seeing her financial history summarized in a single document was daunting. But as she carefully reviewed the report, she felt a sense of empowerment. This was her financial story, and she had the ability to shape it moving forward.

2. **Monitor Your Credit Score**

   To stay on top of her financial health, Adhieu signed up for a credit monitoring service that provided her with regular updates on her credit score. The service also alerted her to any significant changes, such as new accounts being opened in her name or large balances being reported. Knowing that she would be notified if something unusual happened with her credit profile gave her peace of mind.

   Each month, when she received an update on her credit score, she would take a moment to reflect on her progress. Every small improvement in her score felt like a victory, a tangible sign that she was moving in the right direction.

3. **Dispute Errors**

   If she ever found an error on her credit report, the bank advisor had reassured her that she had the right to dispute it. Credit reporting agencies were required to investigate and correct any inaccuracies. Armed with this knowledge, Adhieu felt confident that she could handle any discrepancies that might arise.

   This vigilance paid off one day when she noticed an unfamiliar account on her report. After some investigation, she discovered that it was an error. She promptly disputed it with the credit reporting agency, and within a few weeks, the mistake was corrected. This experience reinforced the importance of regularly reviewing her credit report—it wasn't just about keeping an eye on her score, but also about protecting her financial identity.

3.3 Avoiding Common Pitfalls: A Journey of Discipline

While credit could be a valuable tool, it also came with risks. Adhieu was determined to avoid the common pitfalls that so many people fell into. She had seen firsthand how financial mismanagement could affect people's lives, and she didn't want to repeat those mistakes.

1. **Avoid Excessive Debt**

   One of the biggest risks with credit was accumulating excessive debt. It was easy to borrow more than you could afford to repay, especially when credit was so readily available. Adhieu made a promise to herself that she wouldn't borrow more than she could comfortably repay. She understood that living within her means was essential to maintaining her financial health.

   She recalled the stories she had heard from friends who had fallen into debt traps. Some had taken out multiple credit cards and loans without fully understanding the long-term impact. Adhieu knew that this was a path she wanted to avoid at all costs. She would prioritize careful planning and thoughtful decision-making over impulse spending.

2. **Manage Credit Card Balances**

   Whenever possible, Adhieu paid off her credit card balance in full each month. This helped her avoid interest charges and kept her debt under control. If she couldn't pay the full amount, she made sure to pay more than the minimum to reduce her debt faster. She had heard stories of people who had fallen into the trap of paying only the minimum amount each month, watching as their debt ballooned due to high interest rates. She was determined not to let that happen to her.

   Paying off her credit card became a point of pride for Adhieu. Each time she saw a zero balance at the end of the month, she felt a sense of accomplishment. It wasn't just about avoiding debt—it was about proving to herself that she could handle this new financial system.

3. **Seek Credit Counseling**

Adhieu also learned about credit counseling services. These services provided guidance on budgeting, debt management, and improving credit profiles. If she ever found herself struggling with credit management, she knew that help was available. It was reassuring to know that she didn't have to navigate these challenges alone—there were resources and professionals who could assist her.

While she hadn't needed to use credit counseling services yet, she kept the information in the back of her mind, just in case. After all, life could be unpredictable, and being prepared for anything was a lesson she had learned early on.

3.4 Credit and Loans: Building Towards the Future

As Adhieu's understanding of credit grew, so did her confidence in using it as a tool to build the future she envisioned. Credit wasn't just about borrowing money—it was about creating opportunities. With a good credit score and responsible management, she could access loans that would help her achieve her long-term goals, such as buying a home, starting a business, or furthering her education.

3.4.1 Understanding Loans: A Path to Growth

Loans were another critical part of the financial landscape in Australia. They provided a way to finance larger purchases that she couldn't afford upfront, such as a car, a home, or a business investment. The bank advisor explained the different types of loans available and how each one worked.

1. **Personal Loans**

Personal loans were a flexible option that could be used for a variety of purposes, such as consolidating debt, funding a home renovation, or covering unexpected expenses. These loans typically had fixed interest rates and repayment terms, making them predictable and easier to manage. For Adhieu, a personal loan could be a stepping stone to achieving one of her financial goals, like expanding her skills through further education.

2. **Car Loans**

A car was one of the first major purchases many Australians made using a loan. The bank advisor explained that car loans were typically installment loans with fixed monthly payments over a set period. Owning a car could make life in Australia more convenient, especially when commuting to work or exploring the country. However, Adhieu knew that she would only take out a car loan when she felt financially ready.

3. **Home Loans (Mortgages)**

Buying a home was a dream for many people, including Adhieu. The idea of owning property in Australia seemed like a distant goal, but with the right planning, it was achievable. The bank advisor introduced her to the concept of a mortgage—a long-term loan used to finance the purchase of a home. Mortgages typically had lower interest rates than other types of loans because they were secured by the property. However, they also required a significant commitment, both financially and in terms of time, as most mortgages spanned 25 to 30 years.

"One day," Adhieu thought to herself, "I'll own a home here in Australia." It was a big dream, but with careful planning and responsible credit management, she believed it was possible.

3.4.2 Choosing the Right Loan: A Decision-Making Process

When it came time to apply for a loan, whether for a car, a home, or any other purpose, Adhieu knew that making the right decision was crucial. The bank advisor offered some advice on how to choose the right loan for her needs:

1. **Evaluate Financing Options**

   When considering a loan, it was important to evaluate different financing options. This meant comparing interest rates, loan terms, and repayment schedules from various lenders to find the best deal. Adhieu learned that a higher credit score could help her qualify for lower interest rates, saving her money in the long run. She made a mental note to keep improving her credit score to ensure she could access the best financing options when the time came.

2. **Consider Affordability**

   Just because she was approved for a loan didn't mean she could afford it. Adhieu knew that she needed to carefully consider the monthly payments and ensure they fit within her budget. Taking on too much debt could strain her finances and make it difficult to meet other obligations. She was determined to avoid overextending herself financially, a mistake she had seen others make.

3. **Negotiate Terms**

   The bank advisor also emphasized the importance of negotiation. When applying for a loan, it was possible to negotiate the terms, such as the interest rate or the repayment period, to secure a better deal. Having a strong credit history gave borrowers more leverage in these negotiations. Adhieu felt empowered by this knowledge— no longer would she feel like she had to accept the first offer she received. She would negotiate confidently, knowing that her financial discipline had earned her the right to favorable terms. Negotiation wasn't just about getting a better deal—it was about advocating for herself and ensuring that her financial decisions aligned with her long-term goals.

She remembered the first time she successfully negotiated the interest rate on a small personal loan for an unexpected car repair. It wasn't a significant loan, but securing a lower interest rate gave her confidence. It proved to her that her efforts to build a strong credit profile were paying off.

3.5 Managing Loans During Financial Challenges: Staying Resilient

As confident as she was in her ability to manage credit and loans, Adhieu knew that life could be unpredictable. Even the best-laid financial plans could be disrupted by unexpected challenges, such as a job loss, a medical emergency, or an economic downturn. Being prepared to handle these situations was critical to maintaining financial stability and protecting her credit.

1. **Communicate with Lenders**

    If she ever found herself facing financial difficulties, Adhieu knew that the first step was to communicate with her lenders. Many lenders were willing to work with borrowers to create payment plans, offer temporary relief, or defer payments during difficult times. By being proactive and transparent about her situation, she could avoid late fees, penalties, and damage to her credit score.

    She recalled a time when her hours were cut at work due to an economic downturn. Faced with reduced income, Adhieu quickly reached out to her lender to negotiate a temporary reduction in her loan payments. The lender was understanding and worked with her to create a modified payment plan. This experience taught her the importance of communication and taking action early when financial challenges arose.

2. **Seek Financial Assistance**

   During particularly tough times, such as a job loss or unexpected medical expenses, Adhieu knew that she could explore options for financial assistance. This could include government programs, community resources, or nonprofit organizations that offered help in managing debt and maintaining financial stability. She had seen how community support had been a lifeline for her family in South Sudan, and she knew that similar support existed in Australia, albeit in a different form.

   Adhieu discovered that Australia had a range of financial assistance programs designed to help people through tough times. These programs provided temporary relief, such as unemployment benefits or emergency financial aid. Knowing that these resources were available gave her a sense of security—it was comforting to know that if things ever became overwhelming, there were places she could turn for help.

3. **Review and Adjust Financial Plans**

   Flexibility was key to staying financially resilient. Adhieu regularly reviewed her financial plan to ensure it aligned with her current situation. If her income changed, or if unexpected expenses arose, she would make adjustments to her budget and loan repayment strategies to stay on track. She understood that financial plans weren't static—they needed to adapt to life's changes.

She learned to be proactive rather than reactive. If she noticed that her financial situation was shifting, she would immediately revisit her budget to see where adjustments could be made. This forward-thinking approach helped her avoid financial crises before they escalated. Whether it was cutting back on discretionary spending, adjusting her savings goals, or renegotiating loan terms, Adhieu was always ready to adapt her plan as needed.

3.6 Resources and Tools: Empowering Adhieu's Journey

Throughout her journey, Adhieu discovered several resources and tools that empowered her to make informed financial decisions and manage her credit and loans effectively. These resources became invaluable in helping her stay on top of her finances and navigate the complexities of the Australian financial system.

3.6.1 Credit Reports and Scores

One of the most important tools in Adhieu's financial toolkit was her ability to access and monitor her credit reports and scores. She made it a habit to obtain her credit reports from the major credit reporting agencies in Australia, such as Equifax, Experian, and illion. By regularly reviewing her credit report, she could ensure that all the information was accurate and up to date. This also gave her an opportunity to spot any errors or discrepancies that could negatively impact her credit score.

She also learned to be vigilant about checking for any signs of identity theft or fraud. In an increasingly digital world, personal information was more vulnerable than ever, and staying on top of her credit report helped her protect herself from potential financial harm.

3.6.2 Credit Monitoring Services

To supplement her manual checks, Adhieu signed up for a credit monitoring service. These services provided her with regular updates on her credit score and alerted her to any significant changes, such as new accounts being opened in her name or large balances being reported. This gave her peace of mind, knowing that she would be notified if anything unusual happened with her credit profile.

She also appreciated the convenience of receiving credit score updates on a monthly basis. It allowed her to track her progress and see how her financial decisions were affecting her creditworthiness over time. Each time her credit score improved, she felt a sense of accomplishment—it was tangible proof that her hard work and discipline were paying off.

3.6.3 Financial Planning Resources

In addition to credit-specific tools, Adhieu relied on a range of financial planning resources to help her manage her overall financial life. She found budgeting apps particularly useful for tracking her income and expenses. With a simple tap on her phone, she could see how much she had spent in different categories, like groceries, transportation, and entertainment. This helped her stay within her budget and avoid overspending.

She also explored financial counseling services, which offered personalized advice and guidance on managing debt, saving for the future, and achieving her financial goals. These services were often provided by nonprofit organizations, and Adhieu found their expertise invaluable, especially when she had questions about more complex financial topics.

3.6.4 Government and Community Resources

Adhieu was pleasantly surprised to discover that Australia had a wealth of government and community resources available to help people manage their finances. These resources included online calculators for estimating loan repayments, information on government assistance programs, and workshops on financial literacy.

She attended a few financial literacy workshops hosted by local community organizations, where she learned about topics like superannuation, retirement planning, and tax strategies. These workshops not only provided her with practical knowledge but also connected her with other people in the community who were on similar financial journeys. It was reassuring to know that she wasn't alone in navigating the complexities of the Australian financial system.

3.7 Building Towards the Future: A Credit-Wise Path Forward

Understanding and managing credit had become a cornerstone of Adhieu's financial journey in Australia. She had started out as a newcomer with no knowledge of how credit worked, but through determination, discipline, and the use of the right resources, she had gained the skills and confidence to make credit work for her rather than against her.

As she reflected on her progress, she realized that credit wasn't just about borrowing money—it was about creating opportunities. With a strong credit score and responsible management, she could access loans that would help her achieve her long-term goals, such as buying a home, starting a business, or furthering her education. These dreams no longer felt distant or out of reach. With every step she took, she was getting closer to building the future she envisioned for herself and her family.

One of the most significant lessons she had learned was that financial success wasn't just about earning more money—it was about managing what you had wisely. Credit, when used responsibly, could be a powerful tool for building wealth and achieving financial stability. But it required knowledge, discipline, and careful planning.

3.7.1 Preparing for Major Life Goals

With her newfound confidence in managing credit and loans, Adhieu began to set her sights on some of her larger life goals. These included:

1. **Homeownership:**
    Owning a home was a dream that had always seemed far away, but now, it felt within reach. She knew that building a strong credit profile would be essential when it came time to apply for a mortgage. By continuing to manage her credit responsibly and save for a down payment, she was laying the groundwork for one day owning her own piece of property in Australia.

2. **Starting a Business:**
    Adhieu had always been entrepreneurial, and she dreamed of starting her own business. Whether it was a small retail shop, a catering business, or a consultancy, she knew that access to capital would be crucial to getting her business off the ground. With a good credit score and a solid financial plan, she would be in a strong position to secure a business loan when the time came.

3. **Further Education:**
    Continuing her education was another goal that was close to her heart. Whether it was pursuing a degree in business management or taking courses to improve her skills in a specific area, she knew that further education would open doors to new opportunities. And if she needed to take out a student loan to achieve that goal, she felt confident that she could manage it responsibly.

3.7.2 Long-Term Financial Stability

As much as Adhieu was focused on achieving her immediate goals, she also knew that long-term financial stability was equally important. Building wealth and ensuring financial security for her later years required careful planning and smart financial decisions.

She had already started contributing to her superannuation fund through her employer, but she wanted to take a more active role in managing her retirement savings. She began researching different superannuation funds and investment options, with the goal of maximizing her returns and ensuring that she would have enough saved for a comfortable retirement.

She also began to explore other investment opportunities, such as shares, bonds, and real estate. While these were new and unfamiliar concepts to her, she was eager to learn and expand her financial knowledge. She understood that diversifying her investments was key to building long-term wealth and protecting herself against financial risks.

Conclusion: A Journey of Empowerment

As Adhieu reflected on her journey from South Sudan to Australia, she felt a deep sense of pride in how far she had come. Learning to navigate the world of credit and loans had been challenging at times, but it had also been incredibly empowering. She had gone from having no knowledge of credit to becoming a financially savvy individual who understood how to use credit to her advantage.

Her journey was far from over—there were still many goals to achieve and lessons to learn—but she felt confident in her ability to continue building the future she wanted. By understanding and using credit wisely, she was creating opportunities not only for herself but also for her family, both in Australia and back in South Sudan.

With each step she took, she was laying the foundation for a better future—

one where financial stability and success were within reach. And as she continued on her path, she knew that the lessons she had learned about credit and loans would serve her well for years to come.

The concept of credit had evolved in her mind from a mysterious and intimidating force to a powerful tool that, when used wisely, could open doors to new opportunities. She had built her financial knowledge one step at a time, and now, with each decision she made, she was closer to achieving the dreams she had set out for herself when she first arrived in Australia.

As she prepared for the next stage of her financial journey, Adhieu knew that credit would continue to play a vital role. Whether it was for buying her first home, starting a business, or investing in her education, her ability to manage credit wisely would be key to unlocking these opportunities. And with the skills and confidence she had gained, she felt ready for whatever came next.

FAQs: Key Lessons from Adhieu's Credit and Loan Journey

Q1: What is the difference between revolving and installment credit?

A1: Revolving credit allows you to borrow up to a limit and make payments over time, while installment credit involves borrowing a specific amount and repaying it in fixed installments.

Q2: How can I improve my credit score?

A2: Improve your credit score by paying bills on time, maintaining low credit utilization, diversifying credit accounts, and monitoring your credit report for errors.

Q3: What should I do if I find an error on my credit report?

A3: Dispute errors with the credit reporting agency and provide supporting documentation to correct inaccuracies on your credit report.

Q4: How can I manage credit card debt effectively?

A4: Pay off credit card balances in full each month, make more than the minimum payment if carrying a balance, and avoid accumulating excessive debt.

Q5: Are there resources available for credit counseling?

A5: Yes, credit counseling services provide guidance on budgeting, debt management, and improving your credit profile. Seek assistance if you need help managing credit or debt.

CHAPTER 4

INVESTING FOR THE FUTURE

Introduction: Amsale's Journey into the World of Investing

Amsale stood on the balcony of her small apartment in Perth, watching the sun dip below the horizon. The golden light bathed the skyline, casting long shadows over the city. In that quiet moment, Amsale felt a deep sense of pride mixed with an undercurrent of apprehension. She had come a long way from her homeland of Ethiopia, where life had been filled with challenges she had since overcome. Here in Australia, Amsale had built a new life for herself—working as a nurse, sending money back to her family in Addis Ababa, and finding her footing in this foreign land. But as the days went by, she began to realize something: simply working and saving wasn't enough to secure her future.

Growing up in Ethiopia, Amsale had learned the value of hard work. Her parents had been farmers, and she understood from a young age that every birr mattered. The concept of investing, however, was something she had never considered. In her community, wealth was built through land, livestock, and small businesses. Investments in stocks, bonds, or real estate were distant concepts—things that only wealthy people in big cities did. But now, Amsale was determined to learn how to make her money work for her. She wanted to secure a future not only for herself but also for her younger siblings back in Ethiopia.

Amsale's interest in investing began one evening after a long day at the hospital. She overheard a conversation between two of her colleagues, Sarah and James, as they discussed their investment portfolios. They were talking about dividends, stock market trends, and compound interest—concepts that were foreign to Amsale but intriguing nonetheless. She felt a mixture of curiosity and intimidation. However, as she listened to them, she made a decision: she would learn everything she could about investing. It was a new challenge, but she had faced tougher challenges before. If investing was the key to building wealth and creating opportunities, Amsale was ready to dive in.

That evening, after finishing her shift, Amsale sat down at her kitchen table with her laptop. She began to research the basics of investing, watching videos and reading articles. At first, it was overwhelming—so many new terms, so much information to take in. But Amsale was determined. She had navigated the complexities of migrating to a new country, and she knew that this was just another challenge to overcome. She reminded herself that every journey began with a single step. What initially seemed like a daunting task became a fascinating world where Amsale discovered that investing was more than just a financial activity—it was a way of taking control of her future and creating possibilities she hadn't even imagined.

4.1 The Basics of Investing: A New Perspective

Investing, as Amsale quickly realized, was about making her money grow over time. It was different from saving, which involved putting money aside in a bank account. While saving was essential, especially for emergencies or short-term goals, investing was the key to long-term wealth. As she delved deeper into her research, Amsale began to understand the basic principles of investing.

She found herself fascinated by the stories of ordinary people who had built substantial wealth through consistent investing. Whether it was buying stocks in well-known companies, investing in rental properties, or diversifying through bonds and mutual funds, Amsale saw how investing could transform lives. These were not the stories of the wealthy and elite; these were stories of people like her—people who had worked hard, saved wisely, and invested smartly. They had achieved financial independence, not through luck, but through discipline, patience, and knowledge.

The idea that she could be one of those people—a woman who had come to Australia with nothing more than her skills, her dreams, and her determination—was exhilarating. She imagined a future where she didn't have to worry about sending money home to Ethiopia, where she could afford to buy her own home, and where she could retire comfortably without fear of financial insecurity. Investing, she realized, was not just a path to wealth; it was a path to freedom.

4.1.1 Why Invest?

As Amsale explored further, she discovered the core reasons why investing was essential for achieving financial security and growth.

1. **Wealth Accumulation:**
   Amsale learned that investing could help her grow her wealth over time. By putting her money into assets like stocks, bonds, or real estate, she could earn returns on her investment. Over the years, these returns could compound, leading to significant growth in her investment portfolio. The concept of compound interest fascinated Amsale—it was like planting a seed and watching it grow into a tree, yielding fruit year after year. Each dollar she invested had the potential to grow into much more, creating a sense of excitement about what her future could hold.

2. **Inflation Protection:**
   Amsale had seen how inflation could erode the value of savings back in Ethiopia. People who kept their money in cash found that it bought less and less each year. Investing in assets that appreciated

in value, she learned, could protect her wealth from inflation. This was especially important to her, as she wanted to ensure that her hard-earned savings maintained their value over time. In Australia, where the cost of living continued to rise, she understood that simply saving wasn't enough—she needed to invest to keep pace with inflation and secure her financial future.

3. **Achieving Financial Goals:**

   For Amsale, investing wasn't just about growing wealth—it was about achieving her financial goals. She dreamed of buying a home in Australia, supporting her siblings' education in Ethiopia, and eventually retiring comfortably. Investing could provide the returns needed to reach these goals, turning her dreams into reality. Each goal had its own timeline, and Amsale knew that by investing wisely, she could make these dreams achievable, no matter how distant they seemed.

As Amsale reflected on these reasons, she felt a surge of confidence. She realized that she wasn't just learning about investing; she was building a foundation for a better life. The more she learned, the more empowered she felt. Investing was no longer something mysterious or reserved for the wealthy—it was a tool that she could use to create the life she wanted.

4.1.2 Investment Risk and Return

As Amsale continued her research, she realized that investing wasn't without risks. Every investment carried some level of risk, and the potential return was often proportional to the risk taken. Understanding this relationship between risk and return was crucial for making informed investment decisions. She read stories of people who had lost money by taking on too much risk, but also of those who had grown their wealth by carefully managing their investments. Amsale knew that to succeed, she needed to find the right balance for her own situation.

1. **Risk:**

   Amsale learned that risk referred to the possibility of losing money or experiencing less favorable returns than expected. Different investments carried varying levels of risk—stocks were considered riskier than bonds, for example, because their value could fluctuate more. But with higher risk also came the potential for higher returns. As she delved into the world of finance, she found herself drawn to the idea of calculated risk. Amsale wasn't afraid of risk; she just wanted to understand it. The idea of balancing risk and reward became a central theme in her investment strategy.

2. **Return:**

   Returns were the profits or gains from an investment. They could come in the form of interest, dividends, or capital gains. Amsale learned that while higher returns were attractive, they often came with higher risk. She would need to find a balance between risk and return that suited her financial goals and comfort level. She read about different strategies—some people preferred to take on more risk for the chance of higher returns, while others were more conservative. Amsale knew she needed to find the right strategy for herself, one that would allow her to sleep at night while still growing her wealth.

3. **Risk Tolerance:**

   One of the most important lessons Amsale learned was the concept of risk tolerance. This referred to her ability and willingness to endure fluctuations in the value of her investments. As a naturally cautious person, Amsale knew that she had a lower risk tolerance than some of her colleagues. She would need to assess her financial goals, investment timeline, and comfort level with risk before making any investment decisions. Through introspection and discussions with her financial advisor, Grace, Amsale began to understand her own risk tolerance more clearly. She realized that while she was willing to take some risks, she preferred a more balanced approach that would allow her to grow her wealth steadily over time.

4.2 Types of Investments: Exploring the Options

As Amsale's understanding of investing deepened, she began to explore the different types of investments available to her. She learned that there were various options, each with its own characteristics, risks, and potential returns. Understanding these options would help her build a diversified investment portfolio that aligned with her financial goals.

Amsale decided to take a hands-on approach to learning about different investments. She attended seminars, read books, and even participated in online forums where other investors shared their experiences. She was determined to become knowledgeable and confident in her choices. One weekend, she attended a community workshop on financial literacy, where the speakers broke down complex investment concepts into relatable terms. Sitting in the room with others who were also eager to learn, Amsale felt a sense of camaraderie. She wasn't alone in this journey—many people were trying to navigate the world of investing, just like her. This gave her confidence and made her feel more empowered.

4.2.1 Stocks

Amsale had always imagined that stocks were something only wealthy people dealt with—images of fast-talking brokers in bustling stock exchanges flashed through her mind. However, as she explored further, she learned that stocks were actually an opportunity for anyone willing to invest in the growth of companies. She could own a small piece of a company, a concept that both intimidated and excited her. It wasn't just about making money; it was about being a part of something bigger.

She began by researching well-established companies, ones she recognized from her daily life, like those providing essential services and products. She learned about the stock market, dividends, and the power of compounding returns over time. Although it was daunting at first, she slowly started to feel more comfortable with the idea of investing in stocks.

1. **Overview:**

   Stocks represented ownership in a company. When Amsale bought stocks, she became a shareholder and had a claim on the company's profits. This was an exciting prospect for her—she could own a piece of a successful company and benefit from its growth. She liked the idea of being an investor in companies that aligned with her values and vision of the future. For example, she was particularly interested in companies focused on renewable energy and sustainable practices, which resonated with her sense of responsibility to the planet.

2. **Pros:**

   ◎ **Potential for high returns:** Stocks had the potential to generate significant returns over time, especially if the company performed well.

   ◎ **Dividends:** Some companies paid dividends to their shareholders, providing a regular income stream.

   ◎ **Ownership:** Owning stocks gave Amsale a sense of pride— she was investing in companies that were shaping the future.

3. **Cons:**

   ◎ **Market volatility:** Stocks could be volatile, with their value fluctuating based on market conditions.

   ◎ **Risk of loss:** If the company didn't perform well, Amsale could lose money on her investment.

 ◎ **Requires research:** Investing in stocks required Amsale to research companies and monitor her investments regularly. She knew that this was a commitment, but one she was willing to make for her future.

As Amsale began to invest in stocks, she also realized that the emotional ups and downs of the stock market could be challenging. On days when the market dipped, she felt a pang of anxiety. But she reminded herself that investing was a long-term game, and fluctuations were part of the journey. She learned to manage her emotions and stay focused on her goals.

4.2.2 Bonds

Bonds were another option that appealed to Amsale. Unlike stocks, bonds offered a more predictable return, which aligned with her cautious nature. She liked the idea of lending money to governments or corporations in exchange for regular interest payments. Bonds seemed like a safer bet, especially as she built her investment foundation.

She decided to start with government bonds, as they were considered one of the safest types of investments. Amsale learned that by purchasing bonds, she was essentially lending money to the government, and in return, she would receive periodic interest payments. This steady income appealed to her, especially since it provided a level of stability in her otherwise diversified portfolio.

1. **Overview:**
   Bonds were debt securities issued by governments or corporations. When Amsale bought a bond, she was essentially lending money to the issuer in exchange for periodic interest payments and the return of her principal at maturity. Bonds were considered lower risk than stocks, making them an attractive option for Amsale, who preferred a more cautious approach.

2. **Pros:**

- ◎ **Lower risk:** Bonds were generally considered safer than stocks, making them a good option for risk-averse investors like Amsale.

- ◎ **Regular interest payments:** Bonds provided a steady stream of income through interest payments.

- ◎ **Predictable returns:** Unlike stocks, which could fluctuate in value, bonds offered more predictable returns. Amsale appreciated this predictability, as it provided her with peace of mind.

3. **Cons:**

- ◎ **Lower potential returns:** While bonds were safer, they also offered lower potential returns compared to stocks.

- ◎ **Interest rate risk:** Amsale learned that bond prices could be affected by changes in interest rates—if rates rose, the value of her bonds could decline.

- ◎ **Inflation risk:** Just like savings, the returns from bonds could be eroded by inflation over time.

Amsale found bonds to be a comforting addition to her investment portfolio. They provided her with a sense of security, knowing that even if the stock market experienced a downturn, her bonds would continue to generate income. It was all about balance for her—finding that sweet spot between growth and safety.

4.2.3 Mutual Funds

Mutual funds were another investment option that intrigued Amsale. She liked the idea of pooling her money with other investors to invest in a diversified portfolio of stocks, bonds, or other securities. This seemed like a good way to diversify without having to manage each investment herself.

After attending a financial literacy workshop, Amsale decided to explore mutual funds further. She learned that mutual funds were managed by professional fund managers who made investment decisions on behalf of the investors. This was appealing to her because it meant she could benefit from the expertise of professionals without having to spend all her time researching individual stocks and bonds.

1. **Overview:**

   Mutual funds pool money from multiple investors to invest in a diversified portfolio of stocks, bonds, or other securities. Professional fund managers oversee the investments, making decisions about what to buy and sell.

2. **Pros:**

   ◎ **Diversification:** Mutual funds offered instant diversification, as they invested in a range of assets. This reduced the risk of any single investment impacting the entire portfolio.

   ◎ **Professional management:** The fact that mutual funds were managed by professionals gave Amsale confidence that her investments were in good hands.

   ◎ **Accessibility:** Mutual funds were accessible to smaller investors like Amsale, as they didn't require a large upfront investment.

3. **Cons:**

   ◎ **Management fees:** Mutual funds charged management fees, which could eat into returns over time. Amsale knew she needed to be mindful of these fees when selecting a fund.

   ◎ **Less control:** Unlike individual stocks and bonds, Amsale wouldn't have direct control over the specific investments in a mutual fund.

> ◎ **Potential for lower returns:** Depending on the fund, returns could be lower compared to investing in individual stocks or other higher-risk assets.

Amsale decided to start with a balanced mutual fund that invested in both stocks and bonds. This gave her exposure to different asset classes without requiring her to make all the decisions herself. Over time, as she gained more confidence, she knew she could adjust her strategy and explore more specialized funds.

4.2.4 Exchange-Traded Funds (ETFs)

ETFs were similar to mutual funds but with some key differences that appealed to Amsale's desire for flexibility. ETFs traded on stock exchanges like individual stocks, which meant she could buy and sell them throughout the day. This was different from mutual funds, which were typically bought and sold at the end of the trading day. Amsale liked the idea of having more control over her investments and being able to react quickly if needed.

1. **Overview:**

   ETFs are similar to mutual funds but trade on stock exchanges like individual stocks. They track specific indexes, sectors, or asset classes, making them a versatile investment option.

2. **Pros:**

   > ◎ **Diversification:** Like mutual funds, ETFs provided diversification by investing in a range of assets.

   > ◎ **Lower expense ratios:** ETFs typically had lower expense ratios compared to mutual funds, which meant more of her money was working for her rather than going toward fees.

   > ◎ **Flexibility and liquidity:** Amsale appreciated the flexibility of ETFs—they could be bought and sold throughout the day, giving her more control over her investments.

3. **Cons:**

◎ **Market volatility:** ETFs, like stocks, could be subject to market volatility, which meant their value could fluctuate throughout the day.

◎ **Trading commissions:** While ETFs generally had lower expense ratios, Amsale learned that buying and selling ETFs could incur trading commissions, which could add up over time and reduce overall returns.

◎ **Limited professional management:** Unlike mutual funds, which were actively managed by professionals, many ETFs were passively managed, meaning they simply tracked an index or sector rather than trying to outperform the market.

Amsale decided to incorporate ETFs into her investment strategy, focusing on those that tracked broad market indexes. This gave her exposure to the overall market while keeping her costs low. She saw ETFs as a valuable tool for achieving her long-term financial goals.

4.2.5 Real Estate

Real estate was another intriguing option for Amsale. In Ethiopia, owning land or property was often seen as a way to secure one's future. Here in Australia, real estate could be a source of steady rental income and long-term appreciation. Real estate investments could range from residential properties to commercial or industrial properties.

After saving diligently for several years, Amsale started exploring the idea of purchasing an investment property. She liked the idea of having a tangible asset that could provide rental income and potentially appreciate in value over time. Real estate seemed like a natural extension of her investment strategy, offering both income and growth potential.

1. **Overview:**

Real estate involved investing in properties for rental income or capital appreciation. Investments could include residential, commercial, or industrial properties.

2. **Pros:**

   ◎ **Steady Rental Income:** Real estate could provide a reliable stream of rental income, which appealed to Amsale's need for steady cash flow. She envisioned owning a property where she could rent to tenants and use that income to cover the mortgage and other expenses.

   ◎ **Property Value Appreciation:** Over time, real estate investments could increase in value, offering long-term growth potential. Amsale liked the idea of building equity in a property, knowing that its value would likely rise as the years went by.

   ◎ **Tax Benefits:** In Australia, property investors could take advantage of tax deductions for things like mortgage interest, depreciation, and property management expenses. Amsale appreciated these tax benefits as they could improve her overall returns.

3. **Cons:**

   ◎ **High Initial Investment:** Real estate required a significant upfront investment, including a down payment, closing costs, and ongoing maintenance expenses. This was a hurdle for Amsale, as she needed to ensure she had enough savings to cover these costs.

   ◎ **Property Management Responsibilities:** Owning a rental property meant taking on the responsibilities of a landlord, including finding tenants, handling repairs, and managing the property. Amsale knew that this could be time-consuming and stressful, especially if she had difficult tenants or unexpected maintenance issues.

◎ **Market Fluctuations:** Like any investment, real estate values could fluctuate based on market conditions. Amsale understood that while property values generally increased over time, there were no guarantees, and she needed to be prepared for potential downturns in the housing market.

Amsale decided to move forward cautiously. She spent months researching different neighborhoods, attending property inspections, and speaking with real estate agents. After careful consideration, she eventually purchased a modest apartment in a growing suburb. It wasn't a luxurious property, but it was well-located, and she believed it would attract reliable tenants. When she received her first rent payment, Amsale felt a deep sense of accomplishment. She had taken another step toward securing her financial future.

4.2.6 Commodities

Commodities were a more specialized area of investing, but Amsale was intrigued by the idea of diversifying her portfolio with physical goods like gold, oil, or agricultural products. Investing in commodities involved buying and selling these goods or related financial instruments. While Amsale knew that commodities were often more volatile than other investments, she saw them as a way to further diversify her portfolio and hedge against risks like inflation.

1. **Overview:**
   Commodities are physical goods such as gold, oil, or agricultural products. Investing in commodities involves buying and selling these goods or related financial instruments, such as futures contracts.

2. **Pros:**
   ◎ **Diversification Away from Traditional Assets:**

Commodities provided a way to diversify beyond stocks, bonds, and real estate, offering protection against market volatility in other asset classes.

◎ **Hedge Against Inflation:** Commodities like gold were often seen as a hedge against inflation, as their value tended to rise when the purchasing power of money declined. This appealed to Amsale, who was always mindful of inflation's impact on her savings and investments.

3. **Cons:**

◎ **High Volatility:** Commodities were known for their volatility, with prices subject to rapid changes based on supply and demand, geopolitical events, and market speculation. Amsale knew that this made commodities a riskier investment.

◎ **Specialized Knowledge Required:** Investing in commodities required a deep understanding of the specific markets for those goods. Amsale recognized that she would need to invest time in learning about these markets if she wanted to include commodities in her portfolio.

◎ **Commodity-Specific Risks:** Each commodity had its own unique risks, whether it was the impact of weather on agricultural products, geopolitical tensions affecting oil supplies, or changes in technology reducing demand for certain materials. Amsale knew she needed to be cautious and selective if she chose to invest in commodities.

While commodities weren't a primary focus of her investment strategy, Amsale decided to dip her toes in by purchasing a small amount of gold. She saw it as a way to diversify her portfolio and protect against inflation, without committing too much of her resources to this more volatile asset class.

4.3 Developing an Investment Strategy: Planning for the Future

Armed with knowledge about the different types of investments, Amsale knew that she needed a solid investment strategy tailored to her specific goals and risk tolerance. She had seen too many people back home struggle because they didn't have a plan for their money. She didn't want to fall into the same trap—she wanted to be deliberate and thoughtful about how she invested her hard-earned savings.

Her strategy would need to balance growth with safety, immediate needs with long-term aspirations. She knew that there was no "one-size-fits-all" approach to investing. Everyone's journey was different, shaped by their personal goals, financial situation, and risk tolerance. Amsale spent weeks carefully crafting her investment strategy, knowing that this was the key to achieving her financial dreams.

4.3.1 Setting Financial Goals: A Balanced Approach

Amsale took a reflective approach when setting her financial goals. She thought about her short-term needs, like building an emergency fund and saving for a trip back to Ethiopia to visit her family. These short-term goals required investments that were low-risk and easily accessible, such as a high-yield savings account or short-term bonds. She didn't want to take unnecessary risks with the money she might need soon, so she prioritized safety for her short-term investments.

But Amsale was also thinking ahead. For her medium-term goals, like buying a home or helping her siblings with their education, she was willing to take on a little more risk. She looked at a five- to ten-year timeline and decided that a diversified portfolio, mixing stocks and bonds, would be the best approach. For these goals, she felt confident that balancing risk and return through diversification would yield solid growth.

Her long-term goals, however, required a different strategy. Amsale thought about retirement—a time when she could finally rest and enjoy the fruits of her hard work. She also thought about creating a legacy for her family. These goals required investments focused on growth, such as stocks and real estate. She knew that, with time on her side, she could afford to take on more risk. The prospect of leaving something meaningful behind for her siblings and future generations was a powerful motivator.

4.3.2 Managing Risk: A Thoughtful Strategy

As she crafted her investment plan, Amsale remained mindful of risk management. She knew that growing wealth was important, but preserving it was equally crucial. She decided to adopt several key strategies to manage risk effectively:

1. **Diversification:** Diversifying her investments across different asset classes would help mitigate the impact of any single investment underperforming. Amsale spread her investments across stocks, bonds, real estate, and possibly commodities to ensure that she wasn't overly exposed to one area. She imagined her portfolio as a garden—by planting different seeds, she could ensure that something would always be growing, even if one plant failed to thrive.

2. **Asset Allocation:** Amsale decided that her portfolio should be weighted more heavily toward growth-oriented investments, like stocks, for her long-term goals. For her medium-term goals, she would maintain a balanced mix of stocks and bonds. Finally, for her short-term needs, she would keep a portion of her savings in safer, low-risk investments. This careful asset allocation would allow her to maximize growth while managing risk.

3. **Regular Review and Rebalancing:** Amsale knew that investing wasn't something you could set and forget. She would need to regularly review her portfolio and make adjustments as needed. Market conditions could change, and her life circumstances could shift as well. She planned to rebalance her portfolio periodically to ensure that it remained aligned with her goals and risk tolerance. If her stock investments grew significantly, for example, she would sell a portion of them and reinvest in bonds or real estate to maintain her desired asset allocation.

Rebalancing wasn't always easy, especially when it meant selling off investments that had performed well, but Amsale knew that it was a necessary step in managing risk and ensuring long-term success. The discipline of rebalancing helped her stay on track with her investment strategy and prevented her from taking on more risk than she was comfortable with.

4.3.3 Investment Accounts: Choosing the Right Tools

As Amsale's understanding of investing deepened, she began exploring different types of investment accounts. She knew that choosing the right accounts could have a significant impact on her overall returns, particularly when it came to taxes.

1. **Retirement Accounts:** Amsale had heard about superannuation, Australia's retirement savings system, and she knew that contributing to her superannuation fund was essential for building her retirement nest egg. The tax advantages of superannuation made it an attractive option, and Amsale planned to maximize her contributions to ensure a comfortable retirement. She envisioned a future where she could finally rest, free from financial worries, and maybe even visit her family more frequently.

2. **Taxable Investment Accounts:** In addition to her superannuation, Amsale was considering opening a taxable investment account. While these accounts didn't offer the same tax benefits as superannuation, they provided more flexibility. Amsale liked the idea of having a separate account for her medium-term goals, such as buying a home or funding her siblings' education. She researched different brokerage firms and compared their fees, services, and investment options, ultimately choosing a firm that aligned with her needs.

3. **Education Savings Accounts:** Amsale was also thinking about the future of her younger siblings back in Ethiopia. She had heard about education savings accounts, which offered tax advantages for saving for education expenses. Although education savings accounts like those in the U.S. weren't as common in Australia, Amsale began exploring other ways to save for her siblings' education, such as investing in a portfolio specifically earmarked for their future schooling. She considered setting up a separate investment account, where she could contribute regularly and allow the investments to grow over time. This way, she could help fund their education when the time came.

Education had always been important to Amsale, and she wanted to ensure that her siblings had the opportunities she never had growing up. By investing in their future, she hoped to give them the tools they needed to succeed, whether that meant pursuing higher education or starting their own businesses. Amsale felt a deep sense of responsibility toward her family, and these investments were a way for her to make a lasting impact on their lives.

4.4 Monitoring and Adjusting Investments: Staying on Track

As Amsale's investment journey continued, she understood the importance of staying engaged with her investments. It wasn't enough to simply set up her portfolio and forget about it—she needed to monitor her investments and make adjustments as needed. This wasn't just about maximizing returns; it was about ensuring that her investments remained aligned with her evolving goals and circumstances.

4.4.1 Tracking Performance: Keeping an Eye on Progress

Amsale began by regularly reviewing her investment statements to track performance. She paid attention to key metrics, such as annual returns, risk-adjusted returns, and the overall growth of her portfolio. Monitoring her investments gave her a sense of control and confidence, knowing that she was actively working towards her financial goals.

1. **Investment Statements:**

   Every month, Amsale reviewed her investment statements to ensure that her investments were performing as expected. She checked for any discrepancies and assessed the growth of her portfolio. If any of her investments were underperforming, she made a note to investigate further and consider making adjustments.

2. **Performance Metrics:**

   Amsale also used performance metrics to evaluate the success of her investments. She learned to calculate metrics like the annualized return and the Sharpe ratio, which helped her understand how well her investments were performing relative to their risk. These metrics gave her a clearer picture of her portfolio's health and helped her make informed decisions.

Over time, Amsale developed a routine. Once a quarter, she would sit down with her financial advisor, Grace, to review her portfolio and discuss any necessary changes. Grace had become a valuable partner in Amsale's journey, offering guidance and support as Amsale navigated the complexities of investing. Together, they reviewed market trends, re-evaluated her goals, and made adjustments to her asset allocation as needed.

4.4.2 Making Adjustments: Staying Flexible

As markets fluctuated and her financial situation evolved, Amsale knew that she needed to remain flexible. She had already experienced the ups and downs of life—moving to a new country, navigating a different culture, and starting over. Investing was no different. She needed to be adaptable and willing to make changes when necessary.

1. **Rebalancing:**
   One of the most important adjustments Amsale made was rebalancing her portfolio. Over time, the value of her investments could shift, leading to an imbalance in her asset allocation. By periodically rebalancing—selling assets that had grown in value and buying those that had declined—she could bring her portfolio back in line with her original investment strategy. Rebalancing wasn't always easy, especially when it meant selling off investments that had performed well, but Amsale knew that it was a necessary step in managing risk and ensuring long-term success.

2. **Responding to Market Changes:**
   The financial markets were constantly shifting, and Amsale quickly learned that staying informed about market trends and economic conditions was essential. She made it a habit to follow the news and read financial updates, not to react impulsively to every market dip, but to stay aware of potential opportunities and risks. If there were significant changes in the market, she would assess whether they

warranted any adjustments to her investment strategy. However, she also understood the importance of not panicking during market downturns. Amsale knew that patience was key and that her long-term strategy would pay off over time.

3. **Adapting to Life Changes:**
Life, as Amsale knew too well, was unpredictable. She understood that her financial plan wasn't static; it needed to evolve as her life circumstances changed. Whether it was a new job opportunity, unexpected medical expenses, or a shift in her family's financial needs, Amsale was prepared to adapt her investment strategy accordingly. She was mindful that flexibility was just as important as discipline in her financial journey.

There were moments when Amsale faced difficult decisions—like whether to sell an underperforming stock or continue holding it in the hope of a rebound. She learned to trust her instincts but also to rely on the advice of professionals. Her ability to stay calm and think strategically, even in the face of uncertainty, became one of her greatest strengths as an investor.

4.5 Resources and Tools: Empowering the Investor

Throughout her journey, Amsale made use of a variety of resources and tools that helped her manage her investments more effectively. She knew that having the right information and tools at her disposal was crucial to making informed decisions and staying on track with her financial goals.

4.5.1 Investment Platforms: Finding the Right Fit
Amsale began by exploring different investment platforms. She needed a platform that was user-friendly and aligned with her goals as a beginner investor. After some research and discussions with her financial advisor, Grace, she decided to use an online brokerage platform that allowed her

to invest in a range of assets, from stocks to ETFs to bonds. The platform offered educational resources and tools that helped Amsale understand the intricacies of her investments. It also allowed her to track her portfolio's performance and make adjustments as needed.

Amsale found that the convenience of online platforms made it easier to stay engaged with her investments. She could check her portfolio from her phone during lunch breaks or make trades from the comfort of her home. The platform's educational resources were especially helpful—she frequently accessed tutorials and webinars to deepen her understanding of different investment strategies.

4.5.2 Financial News and Research: Staying Informed

Amsale made it a habit to stay updated with financial news and market trends. She subscribed to reputable financial newsletters and read articles from trusted sources. This helped her stay informed about changes in the global economy, as well as specific developments in the sectors she had invested in. Although she wasn't an expert, Amsale believed in continuous learning and using research to guide her decisions. She learned to differentiate between short-term noise in the market and long-term trends that could impact her investments.

She also joined an online community of investors, where members shared insights and experiences. This sense of community gave Amsale additional confidence, as she was able to ask questions, discuss strategies, and learn from others who were on similar journeys. The support and camaraderie she found in these forums were invaluable, reminding her that she wasn't alone in navigating the challenges of investing.

4.5.3 Professional Advice: Leveraging Expertise

While Amsale had taken the time to educate herself about investing, she also recognized the value of seeking professional advice when needed. She maintained a relationship with Grace, her financial advisor, who provided personalized guidance on her investment strategy. Grace helped Amsale navigate complex financial decisions and gave her the confidence to stay the course during market fluctuations. Having someone with experience to turn to for advice was invaluable for Amsale, especially as she continued to build her portfolio and work toward her financial goals.

Grace had become more than just a financial advisor; she had become a mentor and a trusted guide in Amsale's journey to financial independence. Their conversations often went beyond mere numbers—Grace helped Amsale see the bigger picture, encouraging her to dream big while staying grounded in reality. Grace's mentorship played a crucial role in shaping Amsale's investment philosophy and gave her the confidence to pursue her goals with determination.

Conclusion: A Journey of Growth and Empowerment

Amsale's journey into the world of investing was one of empowerment, resilience, and growth. She had started out as a newcomer to Australia, unsure of how to navigate the complexities of a new financial system. But through determination, education, and the support of her community, she had transformed into a confident investor, actively working toward a brighter financial future.

Investing was no longer a mysterious concept to Amsale. It was a tool that allowed her to take control of her financial destiny, to create opportunities for herself and her family, and to build a life of security and prosperity. Her journey wasn't over—there were still goals to achieve, challenges to overcome, and lessons to learn. But Amsale knew that she was on the right path, and she was ready to continue building her future, one investment at a time.

As she looked out over the city from her balcony, Amsale felt a deep sense of gratitude. She was grateful for the opportunities that had come her way, for the knowledge she had gained, and for the community that had supported her. But most of all, she was grateful for the sense of empowerment that came from taking control of her financial future. Investing wasn't just about money—it was about creating a life of possibility, a life where she could dream, plan, and achieve.

Amsale could envision her future: owning her own home, helping her siblings graduate from university, traveling back to Ethiopia not just for visits but perhaps even to start a small business that would benefit her community. She knew that investing wisely today meant she could live those dreams tomorrow. As she watched the city lights flicker on in the distance, she smiled, knowing she was on her way to something great.

The city lights sparkled like the stars of possibility that Amsale had been reaching for ever since she arrived in Australia. She no longer felt like an outsider in this new land—she had found her place and her purpose. She had learned how to make her money work for her, how to build a secure financial future, and how to invest in the things that mattered most to her. The road ahead wasn't always clear, but she knew she had the tools, knowledge, and support to navigate whatever challenges came her way.

In the coming years, Amsale would continue to refine her investment strategy, adapt to changing markets, and pursue new opportunities. But she never lost sight of the core principles that had guided her from the beginning: patience, discipline, and a willingness to learn. These principles had carried her through the difficult moments, and they would continue to guide her as she built the life she had always dreamed of.

Her story was far from over. As Amsale looked toward the future, she knew that each investment she made was a step toward creating the life she wanted for herself and her family. She was no longer just working for money—her money was working for her, and that made all the difference.

FAQs: Key Lessons from Amsale's Investing Journey

Q1: What is the difference between saving and investing?

A1: Saving involves putting money aside for short-term needs or emergencies, typically in low-risk accounts. Investing involves putting money into assets or ventures with the expectation of generating returns over the long term.

Q2: How can I determine my risk tolerance for investing?

A2: Assess your risk tolerance by considering your financial goals, investment timeline, and comfort level with market fluctuations. A financial advisor can also help evaluate your risk tolerance.

Q3: What is diversification and why is it important?

A3: Diversification involves spreading your investments across different asset classes to reduce risk. It helps mitigate the impact of poor performance in any single investment and balances overall risk.

Q4: How often should I review my investment portfolio?

A4: Review your investment portfolio at least annually or when significant changes occur in your financial situation or market conditions. Regular reviews help ensure your portfolio aligns with your goals.

Q5: What are some common investment mistakes to avoid?

A5: Common investment mistakes include lacking diversification, making impulsive decisions based on market fluctuations, and failing to conduct thorough research. Avoiding these mistakes helps improve investment outcomes.

CHAPTER 5

MANAGING DEBT

Introduction: A Journey to Financial Freedom

Faith Njeri sat at her kitchen table, staring at the stack of bills in front of her. The envelope from the bank, the reminder from her credit card company, and the letter from the utility provider all seemed to blend into one overwhelming blur. The weight of debt had been pressing down on her for years, and now it felt like a mountain she couldn't climb.

Faith had moved to Australia from Kenya a decade ago with dreams of building a better life for herself and her two children. She had imagined that by now she would have bought a home, started a business, and created a secure future for her family. But instead, she found herself buried under the weight of debt, struggling to make ends meet.

Debt wasn't something Faith had anticipated when she first arrived in Australia. She had been careful with her spending, always conscious of living within her means. But life had a way of throwing unexpected challenges at her—medical bills, car repairs, and the costs of raising children had added up over time. Little by little, she had turned to credit cards and personal loans to cover these expenses, thinking she would pay them off soon. But as the years went by, the debt continued to grow, and now it felt like an insurmountable burden.

Faith wasn't alone in her struggle. Many people, especially immigrants, found themselves grappling with debt as they tried to build new lives in foreign countries. The financial system in Australia was different from what Faith was used to in Kenya, and she had made mistakes along the way. But Faith wasn't one to give up easily. She knew that if she wanted to provide a better future for her children, she needed to take control of her finances and find a way to manage her debt.

This chapter follows Faith's journey as she learns to manage and eventually overcome her debt. Along the way, we will explore the different types of debt, strategies for managing debt, and practical tips for improving your financial situation.

5.1 Understanding Debt: Faith's Reality Check

Faith knew that before she could tackle her debt, she needed to understand exactly what she was dealing with. Debt wasn't just one thing—it came in different forms, each with its own terms, risks, and impacts on her financial health. She decided to start by categorizing her debts so she could develop a plan of action.

5.1.1 Types of Debt

Faith's first step was to take inventory of all the different types of debt she had accumulated. As she laid out the bills in front of her, she realized that not all debt was created equal. Understanding the differences between her debts would help her prioritize which ones to tackle first.

1. **Revolving Debt:**
   Faith had a credit card with a significant balance that she had been carrying for several years. Credit cards were a form of revolving debt, which allowed her to borrow up to a certain limit and carry a balance from month to month. While credit cards offered flexibility, the interest rates were high, and the balance had grown faster than she expected. Each month, she made the minimum payment, but it never seemed to make a dent in the total amount owed.

2. **Installment Debt:**

   Faith also had a personal loan she had taken out to cover an unexpected medical expense. Unlike her credit card, this loan had a fixed repayment schedule, with regular monthly payments over a set period. Installment debt, such as personal loans, auto loans, and mortgages, required Faith to make consistent payments until the loan was paid off in full. While the interest rate on her personal loan was lower than her credit card, it was still a significant financial obligation.

3. **Secured Debt:**

   Faith had an auto loan that was secured by her car. Secured debt was backed by collateral, such as a car or home, meaning that if Faith defaulted on her loan, the lender could repossess the car to recover their loss. The thought of losing her car, which she relied on to get to work and take her children to school, added another layer of stress to her financial situation.

4. **Unsecured Debt:**

   Faith's credit card and personal loan were both forms of unsecured debt, meaning they weren't backed by any collateral. Because there was no asset securing the loan, the interest rates were higher to compensate for the lender's increased risk. Faith knew that unsecured debt was more expensive in the long run, so she needed to focus on paying it off as quickly as possible.

5. **Student Loans:**

   Faith had a small student loan from her time at university. Although the interest rate was relatively low, the monthly payments still added to her financial burden. She knew that paying off her student loans would take time, but it was a priority for her because she wanted to free up more of her income for other financial goals.

6. **Medical Debt:**

   The unexpected medical bills that had led Faith to take out a personal loan were another form of debt that weighed heavily on her mind. Medical debt could accumulate quickly, especially if there were ongoing health issues. Faith had learned the hard way that not having adequate health insurance could lead to significant financial strain. She was determined to find a way to manage her medical expenses more effectively in the future.

5.1.2 The Impact of Debt on Financial Health

As Faith reflected on her different types of debt, she realized just how much of an impact it had on her overall financial health. Debt wasn't just about the money she owed—it was affecting every aspect of her life, from her credit score to her mental well-being.

1. **Interest Costs:**

   One of the most frustrating aspects of debt was the amount of money Faith was paying in interest. Every month, a significant portion of her payments went toward interest rather than reducing the principal balance. The high interest rates on her credit card and personal loan meant that she was paying much more than the original amount she had borrowed. Faith knew that if she could reduce her interest costs, she would be able to pay off her debt faster and save money in the long run.

2. **Credit Score:**

   Faith's debt had also taken a toll on her credit score. She had missed a few payments over the years, and her credit utilization was high because she was using a large percentage of her available credit. These factors had negatively impacted her credit score, making it more difficult for her to qualify for favorable borrowing terms in the future. Faith knew that improving her credit score was essential if she wanted to achieve her long-term financial goals, such as buying a home.

3. **Financial Stress:**

Perhaps the most significant impact of debt was the stress it caused. Faith often felt overwhelmed by the weight of her financial obligations, and this stress affected her overall well-being. She found herself losing sleep at night, worrying about how she would make her next payment or what would happen if she faced another unexpected expense. Faith knew that managing her debt effectively was the key to reducing this stress and regaining control of her life.

5.2 Strategies for Managing Debt: Faith's Roadmap to Recovery

Once Faith had a clear understanding of her debt situation, she knew it was time to develop a plan. She couldn't just continue making minimum payments and hope for the best—she needed a strategy to take control of her finances and work toward becoming debt-free.

5.2.1 Assessing Your Debt Situation

Faith's first step was to assess her debt situation in detail. She created a comprehensive list of all her debts, including the balance, interest rate, minimum payment, and due dates. This exercise was eye-opening for Faith—it forced her to confront the full scope of her debt and gave her a sense of clarity about where she stood.

1. **List All Debts:**

Faith listed every debt she had, from her credit card to her auto loan. She included the interest rates and minimum payments for each debt, which helped her see which ones were costing her the most money in interest.

2. **Calculate Total Debt:**

   After listing all her debts, Faith calculated the total amount she owed. The number was higher than she had expected, but it gave her a concrete goal to work toward. Knowing the total amount of debt she needed to pay off helped Faith stay focused and motivated.

3. **Review Your Budget:**

   Faith also reviewed her budget to determine how much she could realistically allocate toward debt repayment. She identified areas where she could reduce her expenses, such as cutting back on dining out and entertainment, and redirected those funds toward her debt payments. Faith knew that every dollar she could free up would bring her closer to becoming debt-free.

5.2.2 Creating a Debt Repayment Plan

With a clear picture of her debt situation, Faith was ready to create a repayment plan. She knew that having a plan would help her stay organized and make steady progress toward her goal of becoming debt-free.

1. **Choose a Repayment Strategy:**

   Faith considered different repayment strategies, such as the debt snowball method and the debt avalanche method. After careful thought, she decided to use the debt avalanche method, which focused on paying off the highest-interest debts first. This strategy made the most sense for Faith because it would help her reduce her interest costs over time. She started by making extra payments on her credit card, which had the highest interest rate, while continuing to make minimum payments on her other debts.

2. **Set Up Automatic Payments:**

   To ensure that she never missed a payment, Faith set up automatic payments for all her debt accounts. Automating her payments helped Faith stay on track and avoid late fees, which could further worsen her financial situation. Faith knew that missing payments would not only increase her debt due to penalties but also negatively impact her credit score. By automating her payments, she could focus on reducing her debt without the constant worry of forgetting a due date.

3. **Allocate Extra Funds Toward Debt:**
   Whenever Faith received extra money, such as a tax refund, bonus from work, or even a small windfall, she made a commitment to put that money directly toward her debt. She resisted the temptation to use the extra funds for discretionary spending and reminded herself that every additional payment brought her one step closer to financial freedom.

4. **Track Your Progress:**
   Faith also decided to track her progress using a debt repayment tracker. Each time she made a payment, she updated her tracker to see how much closer she was to paying off her debt. This visual representation of her progress helped keep her motivated, especially during months when the progress felt slow. Seeing the balances decrease over time gave Faith a sense of accomplishment and reinforced her commitment to becoming debt-free.

5.2.3 Prioritizing Debts: Where to Start

Not all debts are created equal, and Faith knew that prioritizing her debt repayment was key to her success. She decided to focus on the debts that were costing her the most in interest while also considering the impact each debt had on her overall financial health.

1. **High-Interest Debts First:**
   Faith's first priority was her credit card debt, which had the highest interest rate. She understood that paying off high-interest debts

first would save her money in the long run. By tackling the credit card debt head-on, Faith would reduce the amount of interest she was paying each month, which meant that more of her payments would go toward the principal balance.

2. **Secured Debts:**

Next, Faith focused on her secured debt—specifically, her auto loan. She knew that if she fell behind on her payments, the lender could repossess her car, which would be devastating for her and her children. While the interest rate on her auto loan was lower than her credit card, the consequences of not paying were more severe. Faith made sure to stay current on her auto loan payments while also making extra payments on her credit card.

3. **Lower-Interest Debts:**

Finally, Faith prioritized her lower-interest debts, such as her student loans and personal loan. While these debts weren't as urgent, Faith didn't want to ignore them. She continued making the minimum payments on these loans while focusing her extra payments on her higher-interest debts. Once her credit card and auto loan were paid off, Faith planned to redirect those payments toward her student loans and personal loan to accelerate her debt repayment.

5.2.4 Negotiating with Creditors

One of the most challenging but necessary steps Faith took was reaching out to her creditors to negotiate better terms. At first, the idea of calling her credit card company or bank filled her with dread. She feared rejection and didn't want to admit that she was struggling. But Faith knew that in order to make real progress, she needed to be proactive.

1. **Lowering Interest Rates:**

Faith started by calling her credit card company and requesting a lower interest rate. She explained her situation and expressed her commitment to paying off her debt. To her surprise, the representative was willing to work with her. They offered to lower her interest rate, which would reduce the amount of interest she was paying each month. While it wasn't a drastic reduction, every little bit helped, and Faith was grateful for the relief.

2. **Negotiating Payment Plans:**

   Faith also reached out to her personal loan provider to discuss the possibility of adjusting her payment plan. She explained that she was facing financial difficulties and needed more flexibility. The lender offered to extend her repayment term, which lowered her monthly payments. While this meant that she would be in debt for a longer period, it also made her payments more manageable, which helped reduce her stress.

3. **Debt Settlement:**

   In some cases, Faith considered debt settlement as an option. She had read about companies that negotiated with creditors on behalf of borrowers to reduce the total amount of debt owed. However, after doing her research, Faith decided that debt settlement wasn't the right choice for her. She didn't want to damage her credit score further, and she was concerned about the potential fees and risks associated with debt settlement programs. Instead, Faith focused on negotiating directly with her creditors to achieve better terms.

Faith learned that while negotiating with creditors could be uncomfortable, it was worth the effort. By advocating for herself and being honest about her financial situation, she was able to secure better terms that made her debt repayment more manageable.

5.3 Building a Stronger Financial Future: Faith's Road to Recovery

As Faith implemented her debt repayment plan, she began to see progress. Her credit card balance started to shrink, her auto loan was steadily being paid off, and her financial stress was slowly lifting. But Faith knew that managing debt wasn't just about paying off what she owed—it was also about building a stronger financial foundation for the future. She wanted to ensure that she never found herself in this situation again.

5.3.1 Creating an Emergency Fund

One of the key lessons Faith learned from her debt experience was the importance of having an emergency fund. Many of the debts she had accumulated were the result of unexpected expenses—medical bills, car repairs, and other emergencies. Faith realized that if she had an emergency fund in place, she could have avoided relying on credit cards and loans to cover these costs.

1. **Starting Small:**
   Faith started by setting aside a small amount of money each month in a separate savings account. Her goal was to build up an emergency fund that could cover at least three to six months' worth of living expenses. While it was difficult to save money while also paying off debt, Faith understood that having an emergency fund was essential to breaking the cycle of debt.

2. **Prioritizing Savings:**
   As Faith made progress on her debt repayment, she began to prioritize her savings alongside her debt payments. She set up an automatic transfer from her checking account to her emergency fund each month, ensuring that she was consistently building her

savings. Over time, her emergency fund grew, giving her a sense of security and peace of mind.

3. **Avoiding Future Debt:**

   Having an emergency fund in place allowed Faith to avoid future debt. When unexpected expenses came up—such as a medical bill or a car repair—she could use her emergency fund to cover the cost rather than turning to her credit card. This helped Faith stay on track with her debt repayment and prevented her from falling back into the cycle of borrowing.

5.3.2 Improving Credit: Rebuilding What Was Lost

Another important aspect of Faith's financial recovery was improving her credit score. She knew that her credit score had been negatively impacted by her high credit utilization and missed payments, and she wanted to rebuild her credit so that she could achieve her long-term financial goals, such as buying a home.

1. **Paying Bills on Time:**

   Faith made a commitment to pay all her bills on time, every time. She knew that her payment history was one of the most significant factors affecting her credit score, so she made it a priority to stay current on all her payments. By setting up automatic payments and reminders, Faith ensured that she never missed a due date.

2. **Reducing Credit Utilization:**

   As Faith paid down her credit card balance, she also focused on reducing her credit utilization—the percentage of her available credit that she was using. A lower credit utilization ratio would have a positive impact on her credit score. Faith aimed to keep her credit utilization below 30%, which meant that she needed to pay off a significant portion of her credit card debt. As her balance decreased, she began to see gradual improvements in her credit score.

3. **Monitoring Credit Reports:**

Faith also made a habit of monitoring her credit reports regularly. She requested free copies of her credit reports from the major credit bureaus and reviewed them for any errors or discrepancies. If she found any inaccuracies, she disputed them to ensure that her credit report accurately reflected her financial situation. Monitoring her credit reports helped Faith stay on top of her credit and avoid any surprises that could hurt her score.

5.3.3 Seeking Financial Education and Support

Faith knew that in order to build a stronger financial future, she needed to continue learning and seeking support. Managing debt had been a difficult journey, but it had also been a valuable learning experience. Faith was determined to use the lessons she had learned to create a better financial future for herself and her family.

1. **Financial Literacy Programs:**

Faith enrolled in a financial literacy program offered by a local community organization. The program covered topics such as budgeting, saving, investing, and managing debt. Through the program, Faith gained valuable knowledge and skills that helped her make more informed financial decisions. She also connected with other individuals who were going through similar challenges, which provided her with a sense of community and support.

2. **Financial Counseling:**

Faith also sought out financial counseling services to help her navigate her debt repayment journey. A financial counselor worked with her to create a personalized plan for paying off her debt, managing her expenses, and building her savings. The counselor also provided guidance on improving her credit score and preparing for future financial goals, such as buying a home. Having a financial professional in her corner gave Faith the confidence and knowledge she needed to stay on track.

3. **Building a Support Network:**

   In addition to formal financial education and counseling, Faith found support in her community. She connected with other immigrants from Kenya who had faced similar financial challenges. Together, they shared advice, resources, and encouragement as they worked toward their financial goals. Faith realized that she wasn't alone in her journey—there were others who understood her struggles and were willing to offer their support. This network became a crucial part of Faith's financial recovery, helping her stay motivated and providing her with practical advice when she needed it most.

Faith's financial support network also included online communities where she could connect with people who were in similar situations. These forums and social media groups offered a wealth of information, from debt management tips to success stories that inspired Faith to keep pushing forward. Hearing about others who had successfully paid off their debt gave her hope and reinforced the belief that financial freedom was within reach.

5.4 Faith's Turning Point: Debt Freedom in Sight

Months turned into years as Faith diligently worked on her debt repayment plan. Slowly but surely, she saw the results of her hard work. Her credit card balance, once a source of immense stress, was now dwindling. Her personal loan was almost paid off, and her auto loan was down to its last few payments. The sense of freedom she felt as her debt decreased was indescribable. For the first time in years, Faith could breathe easier knowing that her financial future was brightening.

5.4.1 Celebrating Small Wins

One of the strategies that helped Faith stay motivated throughout her journey was celebrating small wins along the way. Paying off a credit card, reducing her overall debt by a certain percentage, or even reaching a milestone in her emergency fund were all reasons to celebrate. Faith treated herself to small, affordable rewards—a nice dinner with her children, a day trip to a nearby beach, or simply taking time to relax with a good book. These celebrations kept her spirits high and reminded her that progress, no matter how slow, was still progress.

5.4.2 The Final Push: Paying Off the Last Debt

As Faith approached the final stretch of her debt repayment journey, she focused all her efforts on paying off her remaining debts. She increased her payments on her personal loan and auto loan, determined to wipe them out as quickly as possible. The day she made the final payment on her auto loan, Faith felt a weight lift off her shoulders. She was now officially free from the burden of secured debt, and her car was fully hers.

Next, Faith tackled her personal loan with the same intensity. Each payment brought her closer to the finish line, and she could see the light at the end of the tunnel. The sense of accomplishment and empowerment that came with paying off her debts fueled her determination to complete the journey.

Finally, after years of hard work, Faith made the last payment on her personal loan. She was debt-free. The moment was surreal—she had spent so long working toward this goal that it almost didn't feel real. But as she looked at her bank account and saw that her money was no longer going toward debt payments, she knew that she had truly achieved something remarkable.

5.5 A New Chapter: Financial Freedom and Beyond

Becoming debt-free was a turning point in Faith's life, but it wasn't the end of her financial journey. With her debts behind her, Faith was now able to focus on building wealth, saving for the future, and achieving her long-term financial goals. She was determined to use the lessons she had learned from managing debt to create a stronger financial foundation for herself and her family.

5.5.1 Investing in the Future

One of the first things Faith did after paying off her debt was to increase her contributions to her superannuation fund. She knew that saving for retirement was crucial, and now that she was debt-free, she could focus more on her long-term financial security. Faith also began exploring other investment options, such as stocks and real estate, to diversify her portfolio and grow her wealth over time.

Faith took the same disciplined approach to investing that she had taken with her debt repayment. She set clear goals, did her research, and made informed decisions. While she knew that investing came with risks, Faith felt confident in her ability to manage those risks and make smart choices for her future.

5.5.2 Teaching Her Children About Money

Faith was determined to pass on the financial lessons she had learned to her children. She didn't want them to go through the same struggles she had faced with debt. She started by teaching them the basics of budgeting, saving, and avoiding unnecessary debt. Faith opened savings accounts for her children and encouraged them to save a portion of their allowance or any money they received as gifts.

As her children grew older, Faith involved them in more complex financial discussions, such as the importance of investing and planning for the future.

She wanted them to have a solid foundation in financial literacy so that they could make smart choices and build their own financial security. Faith's journey had taught her that financial education was one of the most valuable gifts she could give her children.

5.5.3 Giving Back to the Community

Faith also felt a strong desire to give back to the community that had supported her throughout her journey. She became involved in local financial literacy programs, sharing her story and offering advice to others who were struggling with debt. Faith knew that her experience overcoming debt could help others navigate their own financial challenges, and she was eager to make a positive impact.

Faith volunteered at community centers, speaking to groups about budgeting, debt management, and building financial resilience. She also mentored young women who were just starting their financial journeys, offering them guidance and encouragement. Faith's journey had come full circle—she had gone from someone who needed support to someone who was now able to provide that support to others.

Faith's involvement in the community didn't stop with financial literacy programs. She also participated in initiatives that supported immigrant families and helped them navigate the financial system in Australia. Faith knew that many immigrants faced unique challenges when it came to managing their finances, and she wanted to ensure that they had the resources and knowledge they needed to succeed.

5.6 Faith's Legacy: Inspiring Future Generations

Faith's journey of financial empowerment extended beyond just her personal success. As she continued to flourish financially, she became an advocate for financial literacy and empowerment within the Kenyan-Australian community. She believed that her experience overcoming debt could help others who were in similar situations.

Faith began to mentor other Kenyan immigrants who were struggling with debt or financial uncertainty. She organized small financial literacy workshops at local community centers, where she shared her story and practical tips on managing money. The workshops started with just a few attendees, but word spread quickly, and soon, more people were coming to learn from her experiences.

5.6.1 Recognizing the Power of Education

Faith's influence grew as she became more aware of the importance of financial education at an early age. She believed that if people were taught about money management and financial literacy from a young age, they could avoid many of the pitfalls that she and others had experienced. With this in mind, Faith began advocating for financial education to be integrated into the school curriculum.

She started by reaching out to local schools, offering to lead financial literacy workshops for students. The response was overwhelmingly positive. Teachers and administrators recognized the value of teaching students about budgeting, saving, and investing, and they welcomed Faith's involvement. Faith's workshops became a regular part of the curriculum at several schools in the area, giving students the knowledge they needed to make informed financial decisions as they entered adulthood.

Faith knew that by educating future generations about money, she was helping to create a ripple effect of financial empowerment that would extend far beyond her own lifetime. The students she taught would go on to make smart financial choices, and they would pass that knowledge on to their own children. In this way, Faith's legacy would continue to inspire and empower future generations.

5.6.2 Empowering Women in Business

Faith also turned her attention to supporting women entrepreneurs in the Kenyan-Australian community. She knew that many women had dreams of starting their own businesses but lacked the resources and confidence to take the leap. Faith wanted to change that.

She partnered with local business organizations and community groups to create a mentorship program specifically for women entrepreneurs. Through this program, women received guidance on everything from writing a business plan to securing funding to marketing their products and services. Faith also helped connect them with resources, such as small business grants and loans, to help them get started.

The mentorship program was a success, and several women went on to launch their own businesses. Faith was thrilled to see these women thrive, and she continued to support them as they navigated the challenges of entrepreneurship. She knew that by empowering women in business, she was not only helping them achieve financial independence but also contributing to the economic growth of the community.

5.6.3 Leaving a Lasting Legacy

Faith's impact on her community was undeniable. She had gone from being overwhelmed by debt to becoming a leader in financial literacy and empowerment. Her journey was a testament to the power of resilience, education, and community support. But Faith knew that her work was far from over.

As she continued to mentor, teach, and advocate for financial literacy, Faith also began thinking about how she could ensure that her legacy lived on for future generations. She started by documenting her journey and the lessons she had learned in a series of articles and blog posts. These writings became a valuable resource for others who were on their own financial journeys, offering practical advice and inspiration.

Faith also established a scholarship fund for young women in the Kenyan-Australian community who wanted to pursue higher education. The scholarship was designed to support students who were passionate about financial literacy and community service—values that Faith held dear. By investing in the education of these young women, Faith was ensuring that her legacy of empowerment and financial literacy would continue for years to come.

Conclusion: A Journey of Resilience and Empowerment

Faith's journey from debt to financial freedom was a powerful example of what is possible when determination, education, and community support come together. She had overcome significant challenges, built a strong financial foundation, and used her experiences to inspire and empower others. Faith's story didn't end with paying off her debt—it was just the beginning of a new chapter in her life, one filled with purpose, hope, and a desire to uplift her community. Through her workshops, mentorship programs, and advocacy work, Faith made a lasting impact on countless lives.

Her journey serves as a reminder that no matter how difficult the road may seem, financial freedom is achievable. With the right strategies, support, and mindset, anyone can overcome debt, build wealth, and create a future filled with possibilities. Faith's legacy will continue to inspire others for generations to come, showing that resilience, education, and community are the keys to financial empowerment.

Faith's commitment to financial literacy and her determination to uplift others serve as a beacon of hope for those who find themselves in similar situations. Her story proves that it's possible to transform financial struggles into a platform for personal growth and community impact.

FAQs: Lessons from Faith's Journey

Q1: What is the importance of an emergency fund in financial planning?

A1: An emergency fund provides a financial safety net for unexpected expenses, such as medical bills, car repairs, or job loss. It helps prevent the need to rely on credit cards or loans during emergencies, reducing the risk of falling into debt.

Q2: How can I start investing if I'm new to the stock market?

A2: Start small by opening a brokerage account and investing in low-cost index funds, which provide broad market exposure with minimal effort. As you become more comfortable, you can diversify your portfolio with individual stocks and bonds. It's important to educate yourself and invest with a long-term perspective.

Q3: How can giving back to the community benefit my financial journey?

A3: Giving back to the community can create a sense of purpose and fulfillment beyond financial gain. It allows you to use your resources to make a positive impact on others, and it can also provide opportunities for networking, learning, and personal growth.

Q4: How can I continue to build wealth after paying off debt?

A4: After paying off debt, focus on saving, investing, and increasing your income. Contribute to retirement accounts, build an emergency fund, and explore different investment opportunities to grow your wealth over time.

Q5: How can I teach my children about money management?

A5: Start by teaching your children the basics of budgeting, saving, and avoiding debt. Involve them in financial discussions and encourage them to save a portion of their allowance or earnings. As they grow older, introduce them to more complex financial concepts, such as investing and planning for the future.

Faith's story is one of resilience, empowerment, and hope. Through her journey, she learned that financial freedom is not just about paying off debt—it's about building a life filled with possibilities, giving back to the community, and leaving a lasting legacy for future generations.

Faith's journey of financial freedom and empowerment is a testament to what can be achieved through resilience, determination, and a commitment to education. She overcame significant challenges, not only for herself but for her community, inspiring others to take control of their financial futures.

Her story doesn't just end with personal success; it continues to echo through the lives she has touched and the community she has empowered. Faith's efforts to share her knowledge, mentor others, and give back demonstrate that financial freedom is about more than just paying off debt—it's about using your experiences to uplift others, build a supportive community, and leave a lasting legacy.

For those who are just beginning their financial journeys, Faith's story offers hope and practical lessons. No matter where you start, with the right tools, mindset, and support, financial freedom is within reach. And once you achieve that freedom, you have the power to help others do the same, creating a ripple effect of empowerment and financial literacy that can change lives for generations to come.

Faith's legacy is one of hope, education, and community support. She has shown that with persistence and the right knowledge, anyone can overcome financial difficulties and build a brighter future—not just for themselves but for everyone around them.

CHAPTER 6

SAVING FOR MAJOR LIFE GOALS

Introduction: The Beginnings of Independence

Diana Nalubega sat under the shade of a large mango tree on her family's small plot of land on the outskirts of Kampala, Uganda. She had just completed her final exams at secondary school and was filled with a mix of excitement and anxiety about what the future would bring. At 18 years old, Diana was eager to begin her adult life, but she knew that reaching her dreams would require careful planning and saving.

Her dreams were big—she wanted to attend university to study computer science, save enough money to start a small tech business, and eventually help her parents build a better house. Achieving these major life goals would require more than just hard work; it would require financial discipline and a clear savings strategy.

Years later, Diana found herself sitting on the balcony of her apartment in Melbourne, Australia, sipping a cup of tea as she watched the city skyline. It had been over a decade since she left Uganda, and her journey had been anything but straightforward. At 18, Diana had big dreams of attending university, starting a tech business, and helping her family back home. Now, in her thirties, she had achieved many of those dreams—but new challenges and goals had emerged as she built a life in a new country.

This chapter will follow Diana's journey from her teenage years in Uganda to her thirties in Australia as she learns to save for her major life goals.

Through her story, we will explore the practical aspects of setting financial goals, creating a savings plan, and staying disciplined to achieve milestones like buying a home, getting married, raising children, and planning for family holidays.

6.1 The Importance of Saving for Major Life Goals

For Diana, saving wasn't just about financial security—it was about providing her future self and her family with opportunities for a better life. In her twenties, she focused on her education and career, but as she entered her thirties, her priorities began to shift. She knew that achieving her new goals would require careful planning, discipline, and adaptability.

6.1.1 Benefits of Goal-Oriented Saving

As Diana's life evolved, she realized that goal-oriented saving remained just as important as it had been when she was younger. But now, her goals had grown more complex.

1. **Financial Security:**
   By saving for major life goals, Diana could ensure that she was financially secure in both the short and long term. Whether it was building an emergency fund, saving for a down payment on a house, planning for her wedding, or investing in her children's future, having specific goals helped her stay focused.

2. **Achieving Milestones:**
   Diana's goals were no longer just about her—she was now thinking about her future family, her career, and her ability to support her loved ones back in Uganda. Having a structured savings plan allowed her to work toward these milestones without compromising her financial stability.

3. **Peace of Mind:**

One of the biggest advantages of goal-oriented saving was the peace of mind it provided. Knowing that she had a plan in place to achieve her goals helped Diana feel more secure about her future, even as she faced the uncertainties of life in a new country.

6.2 Setting and Prioritizing Major Life Goals

As Diana transitioned into her thirties, she knew that her dreams had evolved. She needed to revisit her goals and create a new plan that reflected her current priorities.

6.2.1 Defining Your Goals

One weekend, as she sat down to review her finances, Diana realized it was time to redefine her major life goals. She asked herself three important questions: What do I want to achieve now? How much will it cost? And when do I want to accomplish it?

1. **Identify Major Goals:**

Diana's first major goal was to buy a home in Melbourne. The real estate market was competitive, but owning property would provide her with long-term stability and an investment for the future. Her second goal was to continue supporting her family in Uganda, particularly helping her younger siblings with their education. Another significant goal that had emerged was finding a life partner, planning a wedding, and eventually raising children. Finally, Diana wanted to start planning for retirement, even though it seemed far off—she knew that the sooner she started, the better.

2. **Determine the Cost:**

Diana researched the costs associated with each of her goals. She estimated that she would need at least 100,000 AUD for a down payment on a house in Melbourne, 30,000 AUD over the next few years to help her siblings with their education, and additional savings for a future wedding, raising children, and family vacations. She also knew she needed to consistently contribute to her superannuation fund to build a comfortable retirement.

3. **Set a Timeline:**

   Next, Diana established a timeline for achieving her goals. She wanted to buy a home within the next five years, continue supporting her siblings' education as needed, and make steady progress toward her retirement goals. As for her personal life, she hoped to find a partner and settle down within the next few years, planning for marriage and children thereafter. By setting specific deadlines, Diana could create a realistic savings plan that aligned with her aspirations.

6.3 Searching for a Partner and Planning for the Future

In her early thirties, Diana began to seriously consider settling down and finding a life partner. After focusing so much of her time and energy on her career and financial goals, she now wanted to build a life with someone who shared her values and dreams for the future.

6.3.1 The Search for a Suitable Partner

Diana had always been a driven and independent woman, but she knew that finding the right partner would enrich her life in ways that financial success couldn't. However, balancing her career, family obligations, and the search for a meaningful relationship wasn't easy. She joined a few online dating platforms and started attending social events to meet new people, but she remained selective, looking for someone who would understand her journey and support her goals.

1. **Defining What She Wanted:**

   Diana took some time to reflect on what she truly wanted in a partner. She realized that she needed someone who was ambitious, kind, and supportive—someone who would not only understand her cultural background but also appreciate the values she held dear. She wanted a partner who was financially responsible and shared her vision for building a secure future together.

2. **Navigating the Dating Scene:**

   Dating in a new country had its challenges. Cultural differences sometimes made it difficult to find common ground, and Diana often found herself explaining her background and the importance of family in her life. But through persistence and patience, she eventually met John, a fellow African immigrant from Ghana who had been living in Australia for over a decade. John worked in finance and shared many of Diana's values and goals. They quickly bonded over their shared experiences as immigrants trying to build a life in a new country, and their relationship grew stronger over time.

3. **Cultural Balancing Act:**

   Diana and John both faced the challenge of balancing their cultural heritage with their new life in Australia. Diana often found herself explaining Ugandan customs and traditions to John, while he did the same with his Ghanaian background. These conversations deepened their connection as they learned more about each other's cultures and found ways to blend their traditions in their life together.

6.4 Wedding Planning and Financial Considerations

After a year of dating, John proposed to Diana during a holiday trip to the Great Ocean Road. It was a beautiful and emotional moment, and Diana felt ready to take the next step in her life. But as much as she wanted to celebrate, she knew that planning a wedding required careful financial consideration.

6.4.1 Setting a Budget for the Wedding

Diana and John sat down together to create a budget for their wedding. They both agreed that they wanted a beautiful celebration with family and friends, but they didn't want to go into debt for a one-day event. They set a budget of 25,000 AUD, which included the venue, catering, attire, and a small honeymoon.

1. **Prioritizing Expenses:**
   Diana and John prioritized their wedding expenses, focusing on what was most important to them. They decided to splurge on a stunning outdoor venue in the Dandenong Ranges, where they could enjoy breathtaking views of the natural landscape. To save money on other aspects of the wedding, they opted for a smaller guest list, choosing to invite only close family and friends. Instead of an extravagant reception, they planned an intimate dinner with quality over quantity in mind. This allowed them to focus their budget on creating a meaningful experience without unnecessary financial strain.

2. **DIY and Cost-Saving Strategies:**
   Diana and John also embraced a few do-it-yourself (DIY) strategies to reduce wedding costs. They enlisted the help of friends and family to assist with decorations, invitations, and even photography. Diana's younger sister, who had a talent for graphic design, created the wedding invitations, while a close friend who was a budding photographer agreed to capture their special day at a discounted rate.

3. **Planning for the Honeymoon:**

    After the wedding, Diana and John wanted to enjoy a relaxing honeymoon. They opted for a budget-friendly trip to New Zealand, where they could explore the stunning landscapes while staying within their means. Diana used her savings from her wedding fund to cover the honeymoon expenses, ensuring they could start their married life without any financial worries.

6.5 Building a Family and Raising Children

With their wedding behind them, Diana and John turned their attention to the future. They both wanted to start a family and knew that raising children would require careful financial planning. They began discussing how they would save for their children's education, ensure their financial security, and create lasting memories through family holidays.

6.5.1 Preparing for Parenthood

Becoming parents was one of the most exciting and daunting milestones in Diana and John's lives. As they prepared for the arrival of their first child, they knew that proper planning would be key to providing a stable and loving environment for their growing family.

1. **Setting Up a Baby Fund:**

    Diana and John created a baby fund to cover the costs of their new addition. They estimated the expenses for prenatal care, delivery, baby gear, and childcare. By setting up a separate savings account specifically for these expenses, they ensured that they could manage the financial impact of parenthood without disrupting their other financial goals.

2. **Parental Leave and Childcare:**

    Diana and John researched their parental leave options and planned how they would handle childcare once Diana returned to work. They decided that John would take a few months of parental leave after the baby was born, allowing Diana to focus on her career. They also explored different childcare options, eventually choosing a local daycare that fit within their budget.

3. **Health Insurance and Education Savings:**

   Diana and John also reviewed their health insurance plans to ensure they had adequate coverage for their growing family. They wanted to be prepared for any medical expenses that might arise. Additionally, they opened an education savings account for their child's future schooling, contributing a small amount each month to ensure they could afford quality education when the time came.

4. **Adjusting to Parenthood:**

   The transition to parenthood brought new challenges for Diana and John. Sleepless nights, balancing work and childcare, and navigating the emotional demands of raising a newborn all tested their patience and resilience. But they supported each other through it all, sharing responsibilities and finding joy in the small moments—like the first time their baby smiled or the peaceful quiet of holding their child in the early morning hours. These moments reminded them of why they had worked so hard to build a stable and loving environment for their family.

6.5.2 Choosing Good Schools for the Children

As their children grew, Diana and John placed a strong emphasis on education. Coming from Uganda and Ghana, where educational opportunities were sometimes limited, they were determined to provide their children with the best schooling possible in Australia.

1. **Researching Schools:**

   Diana spent countless hours researching the best schools in Melbourne, focusing on those with strong academic programs, diverse student bodies, and a supportive environment. She wanted her children to excel academically while also feeling connected to their cultural heritage.

2. **Balancing Cost and Quality:**

   While Diana and John wanted to provide their children with the best education, they also had to balance the cost. They considered both private and public schools, weighing the benefits of each. After careful consideration, they chose a reputable public school that offered an excellent curriculum and a supportive community, allowing them to save money for other future expenses like university tuition.

3. **After-School Programs and Extracurricular Activities:**

   To ensure their children were well-rounded, Diana and John also enrolled them in after-school programs and extracurricular activities. Their daughter, Amina, showed a talent for music and joined the school's music program, while their son, Kwame, enjoyed playing soccer. These activities helped their children develop new skills and build friendships, enriching their overall educational experience.

4. **Cultural Education:**

   Diana and John were also committed to teaching their children about their African heritage. They enrolled them in weekend language classes where they could learn both Luganda and Twi, the languages of their parents' respective countries. They also regularly participated in cultural events in the African community in Melbourne, ensuring that their children grew up with a strong sense of identity and connection to their roots.

6.6 Enjoying Family Holidays and Creating Memories

In addition to their financial goals related to housing, education, and family life, Diana and John prioritized creating lasting memories through family holidays. They both believed that spending quality time together was essential for building a strong family bond.

6.6.1 Planning for Annual Holidays

Diana and John made it a point to plan at least two family holidays each year. These trips gave them a chance to recharge, explore new places, and create lasting memories with their children.

1. **Budgeting for Holidays:**
   Just like their other financial goals, Diana and John set aside a portion of their income for family holidays. They created a travel fund and contributed to it regularly throughout the year. By budgeting for holidays in advance, they avoided the stress of last-minute expenses and could focus on enjoying their time together.

2. **Finding Affordable Travel Options:**
   Diana and John became experts at finding affordable travel options. They often booked flights during off-peak seasons, used travel rewards points, and stayed in budget-friendly accommodations. Whether it was a road trip along the coast or a week-long getaway to Bali, they found ways to make their holidays memorable without breaking the bank.

3. **Creating Family Traditions:**
   Over time, Diana and John developed family traditions around their holidays. Every summer, they would take a road trip to explore different parts of Australia, visiting national parks and camping along the way. In the winter, they often traveled to warmer destinations like Fiji or Bali, where they could relax on the beach and escape the

cold. These trips became an essential part of their family life, giving them the opportunity to bond and create lasting memories.

4. **Exploring Uganda and Ghana:**
   In addition to their trips within Australia, Diana and John made it a priority to take their children back to Uganda and Ghana to visit family and reconnect with their heritage. These trips were a valuable way for their children to understand their cultural roots, build relationships with their extended family, and appreciate the diversity of their background. Diana cherished these moments, watching her children play with their cousins and learn about the places where she and John had grown up.

6.7 Diana's Turning Point: Achieving Her Dreams

As the years passed, Diana's dedication to her savings plan and her commitment to her family began to pay off. Her emergency fund was fully funded, her siblings were making progress in their education, and she had successfully balanced her personal and financial goals.

6.7.1 Buying the Home

One of the most significant moments in Diana's journey came when she and John finally bought their first home in Melbourne. They had saved diligently for years, and when the opportunity arose, they were ready to make their dream a reality. Standing in their new home, Diana felt an overwhelming sense of pride and accomplishment. This wasn't just a house—it was the culmination of years of hard work, planning, and perseverance. The walls of this home echoed with the dreams and aspirations of their future, and Diana knew that it was more than just bricks and mortar—it was the foundation of their family's future.

6.7.2 Supporting Her Family

Diana's commitment to her family back in Uganda remained unwavering. Over the years, she had sent money home to help her siblings with their education, and her efforts were paying off. Her younger brother, Daniel, had just graduated with a degree in engineering, and her sister, Esther, was about to start medical school. Knowing that she had played a role in their success gave Diana immense satisfaction. She saw her family's success as a reflection of her own, a testament to the values of hard work and resilience that had been instilled in her from a young age.

6.7.3 Preparing for Retirement

While retirement was still many years away, Diana felt confident that she was on the right track. Her regular contributions to her superannuation fund, combined with her growing investment portfolio, gave her peace of mind about her financial future. She knew that by starting early, she had set herself up for a comfortable retirement, where she could continue to pursue her passions and enjoy the fruits of her labor.

Diana began to imagine what her retirement might look like—perhaps a return to Uganda to start a community project, or a quiet life in Australia filled with travel and time spent with her grandchildren. Whatever the future held, Diana knew she had the financial security and emotional strength to face it head-on.

Conclusion: The Power of Planning, Perseverance, and the Bonds of Family

Diana's journey from the small village in Uganda to her thriving life in Melbourne is a testament to the strength of the human spirit, the power of family, and the transformative impact of careful planning. She arrived in Australia as a young woman with big dreams, navigating a foreign land while holding tight to the values and traditions that had shaped her in Uganda. But beyond her achievements, Diana's story is about resilience, adaptability, and the unyielding belief that no dream is too big if you're willing to work for it.

Emotional Growth: Balancing Ambition with Family

At the heart of Diana's journey is her emotional growth—learning to balance her ambition with her love for family. Her savings goals weren't just about accumulating wealth; they were about creating a future that reflected the depth of her love and responsibility for those closest to her. Whether it was sending money back to Uganda for her siblings' education or building a life with John and their children, Diana's financial decisions were always tied to the people she cherished.

One of the most profound lessons from Diana's journey is that financial success is not just about reaching personal milestones, but about how those milestones enable you to lift others up. Diana didn't see her success as hers alone; it was shared with her family in Uganda, with John, and with their children. She knew that the financial foundation she was building was one that would impact generations to come.

Perseverance in the Face of Challenges

Diana's story is also a testament to the power of perseverance. The road was not easy—there were moments of doubt, setbacks, and unexpected challenges. When she first arrived in Australia, she faced cultural differences, financial uncertainty, and the loneliness of being far from home. Yet, she never let these obstacles deter her. Instead, Diana learned to navigate them, finding strength in every small victory and using each challenge as an opportunity to grow.

Her journey teaches us that perseverance is about more than just pushing forward; it's about adapting to the circumstances, being open to change, and finding new paths when the old ones are blocked. Diana never lost sight of her dreams, but she also knew when to adjust her plans to fit the reality she was living in. This flexibility, combined with her unwavering determination, was key to her success.

The Importance of Planning and Discipline

Throughout her journey, Diana's story repeatedly underscores the importance of planning and discipline. From her early days in Uganda, where she began saving for her education, to her carefully crafted savings plan in Australia, Diana's life was built on the foundation of clear goals and disciplined action.

She learned that setting specific, achievable goals is the first step to turning dreams into reality. But just as important as setting goals is the discipline to stick to the plan, even when it's difficult. Diana automated her savings, budgeted meticulously, and made sacrifices when necessary—all to ensure that she stayed on track. Her story is a powerful reminder that financial freedom is rarely about sudden windfalls or luck; it's about the consistent, everyday actions that lead to long-term success.

Community and Support: No Journey is Made Alone

Diana's journey also highlights the importance of community and support. While she was incredibly driven and independent, she never walked her path alone. From her family back in Uganda, who inspired her to succeed, to the African community in Melbourne, who provided a sense of belonging and cultural connection, Diana's story shows that having a strong support system is crucial to achieving big goals.

John's role in her life was also pivotal—together, they built a partnership based on shared values and mutual support. Their relationship was a source of strength for Diana, reminding us that finding the right partner can enhance your journey in ways that go beyond financial success. The love, support, and understanding that John provided allowed Diana to reach new heights, both personally and professionally.

In every stage of her journey, Diana's community played a role in helping her succeed. Whether it was her family cheering her on from afar, her friends helping her navigate life in Australia, or John standing by her side, Diana's story is a reminder that no journey is made alone. Success is not just about individual effort; it's about the people who lift you up along the way.

A Legacy of Resilience and Hope

As Diana looks to the future, her story is far from over. The legacy she is building is one of resilience, hope, and unwavering dedication. She has created a foundation not just for herself, but for her children, her extended family, and her community. Every decision she made—from buying her first home to sending her children to school—was rooted in her desire to create a better life for those she loves.

Diana's journey teaches us that success is not just about the goals you achieve, but about the legacy you leave behind. Her resilience in the face of challenges, her commitment to her family, and her careful planning have all contributed to a life that is rich in both meaning and accomplishment. She has shown us that no matter where you start, with the right mindset and support, anything is possible.

Her story is a powerful reminder that financial success is not just about numbers in a bank account—it's about the freedom to build the life you want, the security to support those you love, and the hope to dream even bigger.

As Diana reflects on her journey, she knows that there are still more dreams to chase and new challenges to face. But she is no longer the young girl sitting under the mango tree in Uganda, wondering what her future holds. She is a woman who has built that future with her own hands, step by step, dream by dream. And she is ready for whatever comes next.

Learnings from Diana's Story

Set Clear, Achievable Goals: Diana's journey shows us the importance of setting specific financial goals. Whether it was saving for a home, supporting her siblings' education, or planning for retirement, having clear goals gave her direction and purpose.

Stay Disciplined: Achieving big dreams requires daily discipline. Diana's commitment to saving, budgeting, and planning ahead was key to her success. She automated her savings and stuck to her plan, even when it was challenging.

Be Adaptable: Diana's path wasn't always straightforward, but her ability to adapt to new circumstances and find alternative solutions allowed her to keep moving forward. Flexibility and perseverance go hand in hand on the journey to success.

Value Relationships: Diana's success wasn't just about her—it was also about the people who supported her along the way. From her family in Uganda to her partner John, her community played an essential role in helping her achieve her dreams.

Think Long-Term: Diana always kept her eye on the future, whether she was saving for her children's education or planning for retirement. Thinking long-term helped her make decisions that ensured her financial security and the well-being of her loved ones.

Embrace Your Identity: Diana never lost sight of who she was, even as she built a new life in Australia. She embraced her Ugandan heritage and made it a part of her children's lives, showing that cultural identity is a source of strength and connection.

Diana's story is a powerful testament to the fact that, with determination, support, and careful planning, you can achieve anything—even in the face of adversity.

CHAPTER 7

UNDERSTANDING AND MANAGING TAXES

Introduction: A New Life Down Under

Simba Ndlovu stood on the balcony of his small apartment in Sydney, Australia, watching the early morning light spread across the city. At 27 years old, he was far from home, having left Zimbabwe behind in search of better opportunities and financial security. Growing up in Harare, Simba had seen firsthand how economic instability could wreak havoc on families. His father, once a successful businessman, had struggled to make ends meet after Zimbabwe's hyperinflation wiped out the family's savings. Simba had watched his father's hands tremble as he handed over a small loaf of bread—an entire life's work reduced to nearly nothing.

That image stayed with Simba as he boarded the plane to Australia. He had vowed that when he had the chance, he would build a stable financial future for himself and his loved ones. Now, two years later, he had secured a job as a financial analyst and was determined to make the most of the opportunities Australia offered. But as Simba settled into his new life, he quickly realized that building a secure financial future wasn't just about earning a good salary—it was about understanding and managing the complexities of the Australian tax system. Taxes were unfamiliar territory, and navigating them felt overwhelming at first. But Simba knew that if he wanted to achieve his financial goals, he needed to understand how taxes worked and how to manage them effectively.

7.1 Overview of the Australian Tax System

When Simba first arrived in Australia, the tax system seemed like a maze of unfamiliar terms and rules. In Zimbabwe, taxes had often felt arbitrary, and Simba had never been responsible for filing them himself. Now, as a working professional in Australia, he realized that taxes played a significant role in his financial life. If he didn't manage them properly, they could eat away at his earnings and make it harder for him to reach his financial goals.

7.1.1 Types of Taxes

Simba quickly learned that the Australian tax system was complex, with different types of taxes impacting various aspects of his financial life. He needed to familiarize himself with these taxes to avoid any surprises when tax time rolled around.

1. **Income Tax:**
    Simba's first encounter with the Australian tax system was through income tax. He noticed that a portion of his salary was withheld as Pay-As-You-Go (PAYG) tax. Australia's income tax system is progressive, meaning the more you earn, the higher your tax rate. Simba's salary as a financial analyst placed him in the middle-income tax bracket. He knew he needed to understand how much tax was being taken out of his paycheck and why, so he spent time researching Australia's tax brackets and the PAYG system.

2. **Goods and Services Tax (GST):**
    Simba quickly became familiar with Australia's Goods and Services Tax (GST), which applied to most goods and services. The 10% GST was included in the price of everything from groceries to electronics, and it was something Simba had to factor into his everyday expenses. Unlike in Zimbabwe, where taxes on goods were often unpredictable, Australia's GST was straightforward, but

Simba still made sure to keep track of his spending to manage his budget effectively.

3. **Capital Gains Tax (CGT):**

   After a year of working in Australia, Simba started thinking about investing in property and shares. He had always been interested in growing his wealth through investments, but he soon learned about Capital Gains Tax (CGT). CGT is a tax on the profit made from selling assets, such as property or shares. Simba knew that if he wanted to build an investment portfolio, he needed to understand how CGT worked and factor it into his investment decisions.

4. **Fringe Benefits Tax (FBT):**

   In his second year of working in Australia, Simba's employer offered him a company car as part of his benefits package. While Simba appreciated the convenience, he soon realized that non-cash benefits like a company car were subject to Fringe Benefits Tax (FBT). Although his employer was responsible for paying the tax, Simba knew that understanding how FBT worked was important when evaluating the overall value of his compensation package.

5. **Stamp Duty:**

   One of Simba's long-term goals was to buy a home in Australia. As he began researching the housing market, he learned that buying property involved paying stamp duty—a tax on the transaction of purchasing real estate. Stamp duty varies by state and is based on the value of the property. Simba knew that understanding stamp duty would be crucial when he was ready to take the leap into homeownership.

6. **Superannuation Contributions Tax:**

   One of the things that surprised Simba about working in Australia was the superannuation system. His employer made regular contributions to his super fund, which would eventually provide for his retirement. However, Simba also learned that these contributions were subject to a 15% tax. While superannuation contributions were a long-term benefit, Simba knew that understanding the tax implications of these contributions would help him plan for his future.

7.2 Key Tax Concepts

As Simba settled into his new life in Australia, he realized that understanding key tax concepts would help him make better financial decisions. Taxes weren't just something to pay at the end of the year—they were an ongoing part of his financial planning. By learning about deductions, offsets, and tax returns, Simba knew he could optimize his finances and reduce his tax burden.

7.2.1 Tax Deductions

One of the first things Simba learned about was tax deductions. He discovered that by claiming deductions, he could reduce his taxable income and, ultimately, the amount of tax he owed.

1. **Definition:**
   Tax deductions reduce your taxable income, which in turn reduces the amount of tax you owe. Simba realized that there were various deductions available, depending on his work-related expenses and personal circumstances.

2. **Claiming Deductions:**
   As a financial analyst, Simba often worked from home and used his own laptop and software for certain tasks. He learned that he could claim deductions for these work-related expenses, reducing his taxable income. To ensure he could claim these deductions at

tax time, Simba kept detailed records of his purchases, including receipts and invoices.

3. **Examples of Deductions:**
   Over time, Simba claimed deductions for a range of work-related expenses, including professional development courses, subscriptions to financial publications, and travel expenses for attending conferences. These deductions added up, reducing his tax liability at the end of each financial year.

7.2.2 Tax Offsets and Rebates

In addition to deductions, Simba learned about tax offsets and rebates, which provided a direct reduction in the amount of tax he owed.

1. **Definition:**
   Tax offsets and rebates differ from deductions in that they provide a dollar-for-dollar reduction in your tax liability. Simba was particularly interested in the Low Income Tax Offset (LITO), which reduced the tax burden for lower-income earners. While his income placed him above the threshold for LITO, he was determined to explore all available offsets and rebates that could benefit him.

2. **Types of Offsets and Rebates:**
   Simba discovered that there were several other offsets and rebates available, including the Seniors and Pensioners Tax Offset and the Private Health Insurance Rebate. Although he wasn't eligible for all of them, he made sure to research which offsets applied to his situation.

7.2.3 Tax Returns

Filing a tax return was one of Simba's most important financial tasks each year. He knew that getting it right was essential to avoid penalties and maximize his refund.

1. **Filing a Tax Return:**

   In Australia, most individuals are required to file a tax return each year. Simba learned that this involved reporting his income, deductions, and any tax that had already been paid through PAYG withholding. He was also introduced to myTax, the Australian Taxation Office's (ATO) online service for lodging tax returns.

2. **Lodging Your Tax Return:**

   Simba decided to lodge his tax return online to save time and reduce the risk of errors. He carefully followed the step-by-step instructions provided by myTax, ensuring that he reported all his income accurately and claimed all eligible deductions.

3. **Understanding Your Tax Assessment:**

   After lodging his tax return, Simba received a tax assessment from the ATO. This document outlined his tax liability, including whether he owed additional tax or was due a refund. Simba reviewed the assessment carefully to ensure it accurately reflected his tax situation.

7.3 Strategies for Managing Taxes

As Simba became more familiar with the Australian tax system, he realized that managing his taxes effectively was about more than just filing a return—it was about planning ahead and being strategic.

7.3.1 Tax Planning

One of the key lessons Simba learned was the importance of tax planning. Instead of waiting until the end of the financial year to think about taxes, he started planning ahead to minimize his tax liability.

1. **Plan Ahead:**

   Simba set aside time each quarter to review his financial situation and plan for any upcoming tax obligations. He considered how changes in his income, expenses, and investments could impact his taxes, allowing him to adjust his strategies throughout the year.

2. **Maximize Deductions:**

   Simba made it a point to identify all eligible deductions and claim them to reduce his taxable income. By keeping detailed records of his expenses and staying organized, he ensured that he didn't miss out on any potential savings.

3. **Utilize Tax Offsets:**

   Simba also took advantage of available tax offsets to reduce his overall tax liability. He researched the various offsets he was eligible for and ensured they were applied correctly when lodging his tax return. By being proactive about understanding the tax system, Simba was able to reduce his tax bill and keep more of his hard-earned money.

4. **Plan for Retirement:**

   Simba knew that planning for retirement was a long-term goal, but he also understood that the tax benefits associated with superannuation contributions could provide immediate advantages. He regularly contributed to his superannuation fund, knowing that these contributions were taxed at a lower rate than his regular income. This not only helped him save for the future but also reduced his current tax burden.

7.3.2 Record-Keeping

Good record-keeping became a cornerstone of Simba's tax management strategy. He realized that having organized and accurate records made tax time much less stressful and ensured that he could substantiate any deductions or offsets he claimed.

1. **Keeping Receipts and Invoices:**

   Simba made it a habit to keep every receipt, invoice, and document related to his finances. Whether it was for a work-related purchase, a donation, or an investment, Simba stored these documents in a dedicated folder, both physically and digitally. This meticulous record-keeping paid off when it came time to file his tax return, as he had all the necessary documentation at his fingertips.

2. **Tracking Expenses:**

   Simba also tracked his expenses throughout the year, using a simple spreadsheet to categorize his spending. This not only helped him manage his budget but also allowed him to identify potential deductions and ensure that he was making the most of the tax benefits available to him.

3. **Reviewing Statements:**

   At the end of each month, Simba reviewed his bank and credit card statements to ensure that everything was in order. This helped him catch any discrepancies early and made it easier to reconcile his records when filing his tax return.

7.3.3 Seeking Professional Advice

As Simba's financial situation became more complex, he realized that there were times when seeking professional advice was the best course of action. While he had taken the initiative to educate himself about the Australian tax system, he knew that a tax professional could provide valuable insights and help him navigate any challenges that arose.

1. **Engaging a Tax Agent:**

   After his second year in Australia, Simba decided to engage a registered tax agent to help him file his tax return. While he was confident in his ability to manage his own finances, he knew that a tax agent could ensure that everything was done correctly and that he was taking full advantage of all available deductions and offsets.

2. **Consulting a Financial Planner:**

In addition to a tax agent, Simba also consulted a financial planner to help him with long-term financial planning. The planner provided advice on how to structure his investments, manage his superannuation, and plan for future tax obligations. By seeking professional guidance, Simba was able to make more informed decisions and optimize his financial strategy.

3. **Understanding the Benefits of Professional Advice:**

While hiring a tax agent and financial planner came with a cost, Simba saw it as an investment in his financial future. The peace of mind that came with knowing his taxes were being managed correctly and his finances were on track was well worth the expense.

7.4 Overcoming Challenges in Managing Taxes

Simba's journey wasn't without its challenges. There were times when he felt overwhelmed by the complexities of the tax system or uncertain about the best course of action. However, he learned that staying informed, planning ahead, and seeking help when needed could help him overcome these obstacles.

7.4.1 Dealing with Tax Audits and Disputes

One year, Simba received a letter from the Australian Taxation Office notifying him that his tax return had been selected for an audit. At first, he panicked. The word "audit" conjured images of lengthy investigations and financial penalties. But as he reviewed the letter, Simba realized that the ATO simply needed more information to verify some of the deductions he had claimed.

1. **Staying Calm:**
   Simba took a deep breath and reminded himself that he had nothing to hide. He had kept meticulous records, and he was confident that his deductions were legitimate. Instead of panicking, he contacted his tax agent for advice on how to proceed.

2. **Providing Documentation:**
   Simba promptly gathered all the necessary documentation, including receipts, invoices, and statements that substantiated the deductions in question. His careful record-keeping paid off, as he was able to provide the ATO with everything they needed to resolve the audit quickly and without issue.

3. **Learning from the Experience:**
   While the audit had been stressful, Simba learned an important lesson: being proactive about record-keeping and seeking professional advice could help him navigate even the most challenging tax situations. He also realized that audits weren't something to fear, as long as he was diligent about managing his finances and complying with the law.

7.4.2 Navigating Tax Changes

Over the years, Simba noticed that the Australian tax system wasn't static—tax laws and regulations changed periodically, and it was important to stay informed about these changes to avoid any surprises.

1. **Staying Informed:**
   Simba made it a habit to read financial news and updates from the ATO. He subscribed to newsletters and attended webinars to stay

informed about any changes to the tax system that could impact his finances. By staying up to date, Simba was able to adjust his tax strategies as needed and ensure that he was always in compliance with the latest regulations.

2. **Adapting to New Rules:**
When new tax laws were introduced, Simba worked with his tax agent and financial planner to adapt his financial strategy. For example, when changes were made to superannuation contribution caps, Simba adjusted his contributions to maximize his tax benefits while staying within the legal limits.

3. **Seeking Clarification:**
If Simba ever encountered a tax rule that he didn't fully understand, he didn't hesitate to seek clarification. Whether it was through the ATO's online resources, consultations with his tax agent, or discussions with colleagues, Simba made sure he fully understood the implications of any tax changes before making decisions.

7.5 Simba's Turning Point: Achieving Financial Confidence

After several years in Australia, Simba reached a turning point in his financial journey. He had built a solid foundation of knowledge about the Australian tax system, and his proactive approach to managing his finances was paying off. He felt more confident than ever in his ability to navigate the complexities of taxes, investments, and long-term financial planning.

7.5.1 Buying His First Home

One of the most significant milestones in Simba's journey was buying his first home. After years of careful planning, budgeting, and saving, Simba finally had enough for a down payment on a house in the suburbs of Sydney. The process was daunting, especially when it came to navigating the taxes and fees associated with buying property, such as stamp duty. However, Simba's preparation and understanding of the tax system allowed him to approach the purchase with confidence.

1. **Planning for Stamp Duty:**
   Simba knew that stamp duty would be a significant expense when buying a home, so he had factored it into his savings plan from the beginning. By planning ahead, he was able to cover the cost of stamp duty without depleting his emergency fund or taking on additional debt.

2. **Taking Advantage of First Home Buyer Benefits:**
   As a first-time homebuyer, Simba was eligible for certain government benefits, including stamp duty concessions and grants. He worked with his financial planner to ensure that he took full advantage of these benefits, which made the process of buying his first home more affordable.

3. **Celebrating the Milestone:**
   When Simba finally moved into his new home, it was a moment of immense pride and accomplishment. He knew that this milestone wouldn't have been possible without his careful financial planning and diligent management of taxes. It was a reminder that the hard work he had put into understanding and managing his finances had paid off in a tangible, meaningful way.

7.5.2 Supporting His Family Back Home

Throughout his journey, Simba never lost sight of his responsibility to his family back in Zimbabwe. As his financial situation stabilized, he was able to send money home regularly, helping his parents and siblings with everything from medical expenses to school fees. For Simba, this was one of the most rewarding aspects of his financial success. He wasn't just building a future for himself—he was making a real difference in the lives of the people he loved.

1. **Budgeting for Remittances:**
   Simba made sure to include remittances to his family in his monthly budget. He treated it as a priority, just like his mortgage payments and retirement savings. By being consistent and disciplined, Simba was able to support his family without compromising his own financial stability.

2. **Navigating International Tax Implications:**
   Sending money back to Zimbabwe wasn't always straightforward. Simba had to navigate the international tax implications of remittances, including understanding how exchange rates and transfer fees affected the amount his family received. With the help of his tax agent, Simba ensured that he complied with all relevant tax laws while maximizing the impact of his financial support.

3. **Finding Fulfillment:**
   For Simba, supporting his family was more than just a financial obligation—it was a source of deep personal fulfillment. Every time he received a message from his parents or siblings thanking him for his help, he was reminded of the power of financial stability and what it could achieve. Knowing that his success in Australia allowed his family to thrive back in Zimbabwe filled Simba with pride. It reinforced his commitment to continue managing his finances wisely so that he could keep providing for them while securing his future in Australia.

7.5.3 Preparing for Retirement

Simba was still in his early 30s, but he understood that the earlier he started preparing for retirement, the more secure his future would be. Having seen the financial struggles his father faced during retirement back in Zimbabwe,

Simba was determined not to find himself in a similar situation. He wanted to retire comfortably, knowing that he had made the right decisions along the way.

1. **Superannuation Contributions:**

   Simba consistently contributed to his superannuation fund, taking advantage of employer contributions as well as making voluntary contributions whenever possible. He understood that superannuation offered tax advantages, with contributions taxed at a lower rate than his regular income. This was a long-term investment, but Simba knew that these efforts would pay off when he eventually retired.

2. **Investment Planning:**

   Simba didn't want to rely solely on superannuation for his retirement. He was committed to diversifying his income streams, and that meant investing in property and shares. He had already started building an investment portfolio, balancing high-risk stocks with lower-risk bonds to create a well-rounded strategy. This diversified approach gave him peace of mind, knowing that he was spreading his risk and maximizing his potential returns.

3. **Long-Term Financial Goals:**

   Simba set clear retirement goals: he wanted to retire early enough to enjoy life, travel, and continue supporting his family in Zimbabwe. With the help of his financial planner, Simba regularly reviewed his retirement strategy, adjusting his investment portfolio and contributions as his financial situation changed. His goal was to reach financial independence before the typical retirement age, allowing him to pursue his passions without the pressure of work.

7.5.4 Building a Legacy for Future Generations

Simba's journey wasn't just about his own financial success; it was about leaving a legacy for future generations. He wanted his children and their children to benefit from the hard work he had put into building a stable financial foundation. Simba believed that true financial success meant creating opportunities for others, not just accumulating wealth for himself.

1. **Teaching Financial Literacy:**
    Simba was committed to teaching his future children the importance of financial literacy. He didn't want them to experience the same struggles his family had faced back in Zimbabwe. He envisioned sitting down with them one day, sharing the lessons he had learned about managing money, understanding taxes, and investing for the future. Simba knew that by passing on this knowledge, he could help his children build their own financial independence.

2. **Supporting the Zimbabwean Community in Australia:**
    Simba's success had given him the opportunity to give back to his community. He began volunteering at local organizations that supported Zimbabwean migrants in Australia, offering financial literacy workshops and one-on-one mentorship. For Simba, this was a way to ensure that others didn't have to navigate the complex Australian tax system and financial landscape alone. He knew how difficult it could be to adjust to life in a new country, and he wanted to make that transition easier for others.

3. **Creating Opportunities for Future Generations:**
    Simba's long-term goal was to create opportunities for future generations, both in Australia and Zimbabwe. He began exploring ways to invest in educational programs for young Zimbabweans, believing that education was the key to financial empowerment. Simba wanted to ensure that the next generation had the tools

and knowledge they needed to build successful, financially stable lives. He envisioned setting up a scholarship fund for Zimbabwean students, providing them with the resources they needed to pursue higher education in Australia or Zimbabwe.

7.5.5 Looking to the Future

As Simba reflected on his journey, he felt a deep sense of gratitude for the opportunities Australia had provided. He had come a long way from the young man who had arrived in Sydney with nothing but a suitcase and a dream. Now, he was a homeowner, an investor, and a provider for his family. But more than that, Simba had found a sense of purpose in helping others navigate the challenges he had once faced.

1. **Continuing to Grow:**
   Simba knew that his journey was far from over. There were still financial goals to achieve, investments to make, and lessons to learn. He was committed to continuing his financial education, staying informed about changes in the tax system, and finding new ways to grow his wealth. Simba's story wasn't just about reaching a destination—it was about the ongoing journey of financial empowerment.

2. **Building a Legacy:**
   Simba's ultimate goal was to build a legacy that would last long after he was gone. He wanted his children to look back and see a father who had worked hard not just for himself, but for his family and community. Simba believed that true success was about more than just financial wealth—it was about making a positive impact on the lives of others. And as he looked toward the future, he knew that this legacy of empowerment and resilience would be his greatest achievement.

Conclusion: Simba's Journey of Financial Empowerment

Simba's journey from Zimbabwe to Australia was about more than just learning how to manage taxes or build wealth. It was a journey of resilience, purpose, and growth, driven by a deep desire to create a better life for himself and his family. But at the heart of his story was a fundamental realization: financial success, especially in a new country, begins with understanding the systems that govern it.

The Weight of Responsibility

When Simba left Zimbabwe, he carried more than just a suitcase—he carried the hopes and dreams of his family. The financial instability that had plagued his father's generation became the driving force behind Simba's determination to succeed. He understood that to build a secure future, he had to master the Australian tax system, a complex web that could either work for him or against him. This responsibility wasn't just about survival—it was about thriving in a way that allowed him to give back to the people he loved.

Simba's first encounter with the Australian tax system was overwhelming, but it was also the beginning of his financial empowerment. Taxes were no longer something to fear; they were a tool to be understood and used to his advantage. Through perseverance and education, Simba learned to navigate this system with confidence, turning what had once been a source of anxiety into a stepping stone toward financial freedom.

Learning Resilience Through Adversity

Simba's journey wasn't without its challenges. Navigating the complexities of the Australian tax system was just one of the many hurdles he faced. But each challenge became an opportunity for growth. From dealing with unexpected audits to balancing remittances with his own financial needs, Simba's resilience was tested time and time again.

Understanding taxes became more than just a financial necessity—it became a metaphor for Simba's entire experience in Australia. The tax system, much like his new life, was full of complexities and uncertainties. But by facing it head-on, Simba developed the resilience needed to thrive. He learned that success wasn't about avoiding challenges; it was about confronting them with knowledge, patience, and determination.

Building a Legacy of Empowerment

Simba's journey wasn't just about accumulating wealth—it was about creating a legacy. He knew that his financial success could open doors for others, both in Australia and back home in Zimbabwe. Understanding the tax system was a crucial part of that legacy. By maximizing deductions, planning for the future, and staying informed about tax changes, Simba was able to build a stable foundation that would benefit not just him, but future generations.

Simba's financial empowerment wasn't limited to his own success. He used his knowledge of the Australian tax system to help others navigate their own financial journeys. By volunteering in his community and mentoring new migrants, Simba ensured that his legacy of empowerment would extend far beyond his own achievements. He wanted others to see that financial success was within reach—if they were willing to put in the effort to understand the systems that governed it.

Inspiring Others Through His Journey

Simba's story is a reminder that financial success is about more than just making money—it's about understanding the systems that impact your finances and using that knowledge to create a better life. His journey through the Australian tax system wasn't just a bureaucratic necessity; it was a critical step in his path to financial independence.

For others who, like Simba, have left their home countries in search of new opportunities, his story is a beacon of hope. It shows that while the journey may be difficult, understanding the systems that govern your finances—like taxes—can be a powerful tool in achieving your goals. Simba's success wasn't just about mastering the Australian tax system or building wealth; it was about creating a life filled with purpose, resilience, and a commitment to giving back.

Key Learnings from Simba's Journey

1. **The Importance of Understanding the Tax System:**
   Simba's success was rooted in his commitment to learning the Australian tax system. By understanding taxes, he was able to reduce his financial burden, maximize his wealth, and plan for the future. His story highlights the importance of educating yourself about the systems that impact your finances.

2. **Resilience in the Face of Adversity:**
   Navigating taxes and financial challenges requires resilience. Simba's journey teaches us that while the tax system can be complex, it's something that can be conquered with patience and determination. Every challenge is an opportunity to learn and grow.

3. **Building a Legacy Through Knowledge:**
   Simba's financial success wasn't just about accumulating wealth—it was about using his knowledge of the tax system to create opportunities for others. By sharing what he learned, he empowered his family and his community to navigate their own financial journeys.

4. **Giving Back to the Community:**
   Simba's story shows that true financial success includes giving back. Whether it's through mentoring, volunteering, or supporting others, helping those who are just starting their journey is one of the most meaningful ways to use your success.

5. **Planning for the Future:**

Simba's commitment to long-term planning, including understanding taxes, superannuation, and investments, allowed him to build a secure financial future. His story reminds us that successful financial planning requires both short-term discipline and long-term vision.

Simba's journey is about more than just navigating the Australian tax system—it's about perseverance, community, and legacy. His story inspires us to embrace the challenges we face, educate ourselves, and use our success to create a positive impact on the world around us. As you navigate your own financial path, may Simba's journey remind you that with knowledge, resilience, and a commitment to helping others, anything is possible.

CHAPTER 8

RETIREMENT PLANNING, SUPERANNUATION, AND ESTATE PLANNING

Introduction: A Legacy Beyond Retirement

Ava Uwimana had always been a dreamer. Growing up in Kigali, Rwanda, she often imagined a future where she could provide for her family, travel the world, and retire without the constant worry of making ends meet. But life was never easy. Her parents worked tirelessly to support their children, but financial security always seemed just out of reach. Ava's dreams of a comfortable future, however, remained alive. She was determined to change her family's story.

When Ava moved to Australia in her early 20s, she quickly realized that achieving her dreams would require more than just hard work—it would require careful planning, financial education, and a deep understanding of the systems that could support her. Over the years, Ava learned about superannuation, investments, and eventually, estate planning. But her journey wasn't just about numbers and financial products—it was about securing a future filled with peace, love, and legacy.

Ava's story is not just about accumulating wealth; it's about how a young woman from Rwanda learned to take control of her financial future and create a legacy that would benefit generations to come. Her story will guide us through the complexities of retirement planning, superannuation, and estate planning, highlighting the emotional and practical aspects of these critical topics. Ava's decisions weren't just about securing her own future;

they were about leaving a lasting impact on her loved ones and ensuring that her hard work would benefit generations to come.

8.1 Understanding Superannuation: The Key to Ava's Future

Superannuation was a foreign concept to Ava when she first arrived in Australia. Back in Rwanda, saving for the future had always been a challenge, and formal retirement systems were often inaccessible to families like hers. But in Australia, Ava saw an opportunity. Superannuation offered a way to build a future she could count on—a future where she could retire comfortably and provide for her family.

Ava was introduced to superannuation during her first job at a local café in Sydney. Her employer explained that a portion of her earnings would be contributed to a super fund. At first, Ava didn't fully understand the significance of this contribution, but as she learned more about Australia's retirement system, she began to see superannuation as the foundation of her future financial security.

8.1.1 What is Superannuation?

Superannuation, or "super," became the cornerstone of Ava's financial strategy. In Australia, superannuation is a compulsory savings system where employers contribute a portion of their employees' earnings into a super fund. Over time, these contributions, along with investment returns, grow into a substantial retirement fund.

For Ava, superannuation was more than just a mandatory deduction from her paycheck—it was the foundation of her retirement dreams. Each contribution represented a step closer to the life she had always envisioned.

The more she learned about super, the more empowered she felt to take control of her future.

Superannuation works as a long-term savings plan, with funds generally inaccessible until retirement age. Ava realized that this forced saving was beneficial—without it, she might have spent her income on immediate needs and desires, neglecting her future security. With superannuation, her future was being looked after, even as she focused on the present.

8.1.2 Superannuation as Part of Estate Planning

As Ava became more knowledgeable about retirement planning, she realized that superannuation wasn't just about her own future—it was also about the future of her family. Ava learned that superannuation didn't automatically form part of her estate upon death. Instead, it was held in trust and distributed according to specific rules. This revelation led Ava to think carefully about how she wanted her super to be distributed.

1. **Nominating Beneficiaries:**

    Ava's first step was to nominate beneficiaries for her superannuation. She had worked hard for every dollar in her super fund, and she wanted to ensure that her family would benefit from it if anything happened to her. With the help of her financial advisor, Ava made a binding nomination, ensuring that her superannuation would go directly to her siblings.

    This decision wasn't just about money—it was about love and responsibility. Ava wanted to make sure that her siblings, who had supported her in so many ways, would be taken care of if she wasn't there to do it herself. Ava thought back to her younger brother, Emmanuel, who had always looked up to her. She wanted to make sure that, even in her absence, he would have the resources to pursue his education and build a life of his own.

2. **Considering Tax Implications:**

Ava also had to consider the tax implications of her superannuation benefits. She learned that non-dependent beneficiaries, such as her siblings, could be taxed on the super payout. This led Ava to explore ways to minimize the tax burden on her family, such as considering life insurance policies or establishing trusts.

Tax planning was a daunting task, but Ava knew it was essential. She didn't want her family to be burdened with unnecessary taxes after her death. By making these decisions now, Ava could protect her loved ones from financial stress in the future. She also sought advice on whether she should consider nominating her future spouse or children as beneficiaries if her circumstances changed.

Through these decisions, Ava was able to protect her legacy while ensuring that her family would benefit from the financial security she had worked so hard to build.

8.2 Retirement Planning: Crafting a Comfortable Future

Retirement planning wasn't just about saving money for Ava—it was about creating a life that reflected her values, dreams, and aspirations. She wanted to retire comfortably, travel, and enjoy the fruits of her labor, but she also wanted to ensure that her loved ones were taken care of. Ava's retirement planning journey became a delicate balance of personal fulfillment and responsibility to her family.

Ava often imagined her retirement as a time when she could travel back to Rwanda to reconnect with her roots, visit places she had never seen, and spend quality time with her family. But she knew that these dreams would only become a reality if she carefully planned for her financial future.

8.2.1 Contributing to Superannuation: Laying the Foundation

Ava's contributions to her superannuation were the foundation of her retirement plan. While the mandatory contributions from her employer were a good start, Ava knew she needed to do more. She was determined to build a retirement fund that would allow her to live the life she had always dreamed of.

1. **Voluntary Contributions:**

   Ava made the decision to boost her retirement savings by making voluntary contributions to her super. Through salary sacrifice, she directed a portion of her pre-tax income into her super fund. This not only increased her retirement savings but also reduced her taxable income—giving her more financial flexibility in the present. Voluntary contributions became a regular part of Ava's financial routine. She viewed these contributions not as a sacrifice, but as an investment in her future. Each time she contributed to her super, she felt a sense of pride in her ability to take control of her financial destiny.

2. **Government Co-Contributions:**

   Ava also took advantage of the government's co-contribution scheme. As someone with fluctuating income during her years of part-time study and work, Ava qualified for these additional contributions. Each time the government added to her super, Ava felt a renewed sense of motivation. It was as if the system was rewarding her for her hard work and discipline.

   These contributions weren't just about securing her future—they were acts of hope. Ava believed in a better future for herself and her family, and every dollar she contributed to her super fund was a step closer to that future.

Through these contributions, Ava gradually built up her super balance. She learned that even small, regular contributions could make a significant difference over time. Her superannuation became the foundation of her retirement plan, giving her the confidence to dream big for the future.

8.2.2 Investing for Retirement: Maximizing Superannuation Returns

Ava understood that simply contributing to her super wasn't enough—she needed to make sure her money was working for her. With the help of her financial advisor, Ava developed an investment strategy that aligned with her long-term goals.

1. **Growth-Oriented Investments:**

   Given her relatively young age, Ava opted for a growth-oriented investment strategy that focused on shares and property. These assets carried higher risks, but they also offered the potential for higher returns. Ava was willing to take these risks because she had time on her side.

   Ava's investment strategy wasn't just about numbers—it was about belief in the future. She believed that by taking calculated risks now, she could secure a more comfortable retirement later. She viewed her investments as seeds that, with time and care, would grow into a bountiful harvest.

2. **Regular Reviews and Adjustments:**

   Ava made it a priority to review her investment portfolio regularly. She knew that markets were unpredictable, and what worked a few years ago might not be the best strategy going forward. Regular reviews allowed Ava to make informed decisions and adjust her strategy as needed.

   These reviews became moments of reflection for Ava. Each time she saw her super balance grow, she felt a sense of pride and accomplishment. Her hard work and careful planning were paying off, and she was one step closer to the future she had always dreamed of. By staying engaged with her investments, Ava ensured that her money continued to work for her, even as she navigated the challenges of life.

8.3 Estate Planning: Protecting Ava's Legacy

As Ava delved deeper into retirement planning, she realized that estate planning was an essential part of the process. It wasn't enough to build a secure financial future—she needed to protect that future and ensure that her hard-earned wealth would be passed on to her loved ones in the way she intended. Estate planning became an emotional journey for Ava. It forced her to confront the reality of her mortality and think about what she wanted to leave behind. But it also gave her a sense of peace, knowing that she was taking steps to protect her family and ensure that her legacy would live on.

Ava had seen firsthand how a lack of estate planning could lead to confusion, conflict, and financial strain for families. When her uncle in Rwanda passed away unexpectedly, the absence of a will led to disputes over his assets and created rifts in the family. Ava was determined to avoid such a situation for her own family. She wanted to make sure that her wealth would be distributed according to her wishes and that her loved ones would be taken care of after her passing.

8.3.1 Creating a Will: Ensuring Her Wishes Are Honored

The first step in Ava's estate planning journey was creating a will. She knew that without a will, her assets could be distributed in ways that didn't align with her wishes. Creating a will was an act of love for Ava—it was her way of ensuring that her family would be taken care of after she was gone.

1. **Appointing Executors:**

   Ava carefully considered who she wanted to appoint as executors of her will. She needed to choose people she trusted to carry out her wishes and handle the complexities of estate administration. This decision was deeply personal for Ava, as she wanted to ensure that her family would be supported during what would undoubtedly be a difficult time.

   Ava decided to appoint her close friend Grace, who had been like a sister to her since their university days, as one of her executors. Grace had always been reliable and level-headed, and Ava knew she could trust her to manage her estate with care and integrity.

2. **Designating Beneficiaries:**

   Ava faced another important decision—who would benefit from her estate? She decided to designate her siblings as her primary beneficiaries, ensuring that her wealth would continue to support her family even after her death. But Ava also wanted to leave a lasting impact on future generations. She allocated a portion of her estate to be used for her nieces and nephews' education, giving them the opportunities she had worked so hard to create for herself. Ava's estate planning was about more than just money—it was about leaving a legacy. She wanted her wealth to continue making a difference in the lives of her loved ones, and her will was the key to ensuring that her wishes would be honored. Ava envisioned a future where her nieces and nephews could attend university without financial burden, where her family could thrive even in her absence.

8.3.2 Establishing Trusts: Protecting Her Legacy

As Ava's wealth grew, she realized that she needed to think beyond a simple will. She began exploring the idea of establishing trusts to protect her assets and ensure that her wealth would be used in a way that aligned with her values. Trusts offered a way to provide for her family while also preserving her legacy for future generations.

1. **Educational Trusts for Future Generations:**
   Ava decided to set up an educational trust for her nieces and nephews. This trust would cover their educational expenses, ensuring that they could pursue higher education without the financial strain that she had experienced. Ava believed that education was the key to breaking the cycle of poverty and creating opportunities for future generations.

2. **Charitable Trusts:**
   Ava also wanted to give back to the community that had supported her throughout her journey. She established a charitable trust to fund education initiatives in Rwanda, focusing on programs that empowered young women. Ava knew that her success was built on the support and sacrifices of others, and she wanted to pay that forward by helping the next generation achieve their dreams.

   These trusts were Ava's way of ensuring that her legacy would continue long after she was gone. They represented her commitment to her family, her community, and the values that had guided her throughout her life.

8.3.3 Long-Term Care and Health Planning

Ava's estate planning journey also made her consider her own long-term care needs. As she approached her late 40s, she knew that preparing for potential health challenges was an important part of securing her future. She wanted to ensure that she would have access to quality care if she needed it, without placing a financial burden on her family.

1. **Health and Disability Insurance:**
   Ava reviewed her health and disability insurance policies to make

sure they provided adequate coverage. She also explored options for long-term care insurance, which would help cover the costs of assisted living or nursing care if she ever required it.

2. **Advanced Directives:**

Ava also took the time to create advanced directives, outlining her wishes for medical treatment in the event that she became unable to make decisions for herself. She didn't want her family to face the burden of making difficult medical decisions on her behalf, and she wanted to ensure that her wishes were respected.

8.4 Estate Planning: Ensuring a Lasting Impact

As Ava's life journey progressed, her thoughts increasingly turned to the idea of legacy—not just in terms of wealth, but in terms of impact. Ava wanted to ensure that the wealth she had accumulated would benefit her family and her community in ways that aligned with her values and her vision for the future.

Through careful estate planning, Ava ensured that her wealth would continue to provide for her family even after her passing. She established a legacy that reflected her commitment to education, empowerment, and giving back to the community. Ava's story reminds us that estate planning isn't just about managing assets—it's about ensuring that our values and our impact continue long after we are gone.

8.4.1 Communicating Her Plans with Loved Ones

Ava knew that transparency was key to a successful estate plan. She made sure to communicate her plans with her family, discussing her will, her trusts, and her wishes with her siblings and beneficiaries. This open communication helped prevent misunderstandings and ensured that her family would be prepared to carry out her wishes.

Ava's decision to discuss her estate plans with her family wasn't easy. Talking about death and money can be uncomfortable, but Ava believed that it was necessary to avoid future conflicts. She wanted her family to understand her decisions and to feel empowered to honor her legacy.

8.4.2 Regularly Reviewing and Updating Her Plan

Ava also recognized the importance of regularly reviewing and updating her estate plan. Life circumstances change, and Ava wanted to make sure that her estate plan continued to reflect her wishes as her family grew and her financial situation evolved. She scheduled regular meetings with her financial advisor to review her will, her trusts, and her investments.

By staying proactive about her estate planning, Ava ensured that her legacy would remain aligned with her values and her vision for the future. She knew that planning for the future was an ongoing process, and she was committed to making sure that her estate plan would continue to protect her family and her legacy for years to come.

Conclusion: Ava's Legacy of Love, Security, and Empowerment

Ava's journey from Kigali to Australia is a testament to the power of resilience, careful planning, and a deep commitment to her family's well-being. Throughout her life, Ava faced countless challenges—from navigating a foreign financial system to balancing the needs of her loved ones back home. But through it all, she remained focused on her dreams of creating a better future for herself and those she loved. Her financial journey—encompassing retirement planning, superannuation, and estate planning—was about far more than accumulating wealth. It was about securing a legacy of love, care, and empowerment.

As Ava approached retirement, she reflected on the choices she had made and the lessons she had learned. Retirement planning wasn't just about ensuring she had enough money to live on—it was about creating a life that allowed her to thrive in her golden years. By taking control of her superannuation, investing wisely, and making thoughtful decisions about her future, Ava ensured that she could retire with confidence and peace of mind.

But Ava's story goes beyond her own retirement. She understood that her financial decisions would have a lasting impact on her family and future generations. By carefully planning her estate, Ava ensured that her hard-earned wealth would be passed on to her loved ones in a way that reflected her values and priorities. She wanted her legacy to be one of security, opportunity, and empowerment—and she took the necessary steps to make that a reality.

Ava's journey is a powerful reminder that financial planning is about more than just money—it's about creating a future that reflects your values, supports your loved ones, and leaves a lasting impact.

Lessons for the Readers:

1. **Start Planning Early:**
   Ava's story shows us the importance of starting early when it comes to retirement and estate planning. Whether you're just beginning your career or nearing retirement, it's never too soon—or too late—to take control of your financial future. The earlier you start, the more time you have to grow your wealth, make informed decisions, and create a secure foundation for yourself and your family.

2. **Understand Your Superannuation:**
   Superannuation is a powerful tool for building wealth and securing your retirement. Like Ava, it's essential to understand how your super works, the different investment options available to you,

and how to maximize your contributions. Regularly reviewing your superannuation can help you stay on track and make adjustments as needed to align with your retirement goals.

3. **Think Beyond Yourself:**

Ava's journey reminds us that financial planning isn't just about securing our own futures—it's about thinking beyond ourselves and considering the impact our decisions will have on our loved ones. Estate planning is a crucial step in ensuring that your wealth is distributed according to your wishes and that your family is taken care of after you're gone. By taking the time to create a will, designate beneficiaries, and manage your assets, you can protect your legacy and provide for the people who matter most. Estate planning is not just about avoiding legal complications—it's about ensuring that your values and your life's work continue to make a positive impact on your loved ones and community.

4. **Seek Professional Advice:**

Ava didn't navigate her financial journey alone—she sought the help of financial advisors, estate planners, and legal professionals to ensure that her decisions were informed and strategic. Seeking professional advice can help you optimize your retirement and estate plans, ensuring that your money is working for you in the best possible way. Trusted experts can provide personalized advice, helping you navigate complex legal and financial landscapes with confidence.

5. **Be Resilient and Stay Focused:**

Ava's resilience was the key to her success. Life threw many challenges her way, but she remained focused on her goals and stayed disciplined in her approach. Her story teaches us that setbacks are a natural part of life, but with determination, careful planning, and the right support, we can overcome them and build the future we want. Financial planning requires patience and perseverance, but the rewards are worth the effort.

6. **Create a Legacy of Empowerment:**

   Ava's ultimate goal wasn't just financial security—it was empowerment. She wanted to leave a legacy that would continue to empower her family and future generations. Whether it's through education, opportunities, or financial support, think about the legacy you want to leave behind and how your financial decisions today can help create that legacy. Empowerment is about more than money—it's about passing on the tools, knowledge, and opportunities that will allow others to thrive.

Ava's story is a powerful reminder that financial planning is about more than just securing a comfortable retirement. It's about taking control of your future, protecting your loved ones, and leaving a lasting legacy that reflects your values. No matter where you start, you have the power to build a secure and meaningful future for yourself and the people you care about.

As you embark on your own financial journey, remember Ava's lessons. Take control of your superannuation, plan for your retirement, protect your legacy, and never stop believing in the future you want to create. By doing so, you can ensure that your hard work and sacrifices will continue to benefit those you love for generations to come.

CHAPTER 9

NAVIGATING FINANCIAL CHALLENGES AND PLANNING FOR THE FUTURE

Introduction: The Unseen Battles We All Face

In life, financial challenges are inevitable, and how we navigate them can define our future. But financial stability doesn't happen by accident. It takes planning, resilience, and, often, a community of support. Whether it's the stress of mounting debt, the fear of unexpected expenses, or the uncertainty of navigating a new financial system, every individual has their own financial journey, filled with hurdles to overcome.

This chapter brings together the stories of six individuals—Deng, John, Faith, Diana, Simba, and Ava—who all faced unique financial challenges after migrating to Australia. Their journeys, while different, share common threads of perseverance, hope, and strategic planning. Through their experiences, we explore how to manage debt, prepare for unexpected expenses, and plan for a secure future. More than just about numbers and budgets, this chapter delves into the emotional aspects of financial challenges and how these six individuals overcame them, each in their own way.

9.1 Identifying Common Financial Challenges: The Weight of the World

When Deng first arrived in Australia from South Sudan, he carried the weight of his family's expectations. Back home, he was seen as the one who would make it, the one who could lift his family out of poverty. But the reality of life in Australia was harsher than he imagined. Deng found himself juggling part-time jobs while studying, all the while sending money back to support his family. The weight of responsibility felt crushing, and his finances were stretched to the limit.

John, who had migrated from Kenya, faced a different challenge. As his family grew, so did his financial responsibilities. Providing for his wife and children in a foreign land was no small feat. John worked tirelessly, but despite his efforts, he found himself trapped in a cycle of debt. Credit cards, personal loans, and everyday expenses piled up, and John struggled to keep his head above water.

Faith, a single mother from Ethiopia, faced the challenge of balancing her financial responsibilities while raising her young son. She had to navigate the complexities of managing household expenses on a single income while ensuring her son had access to the best opportunities. For Faith, every dollar counted, and unexpected expenses, like medical bills or school fees, could throw her budget into disarray.

Diana, originally from Uganda, came to Australia with big dreams of building a successful career and creating a life of stability. However, she quickly realized that financial stability wasn't something that happened overnight. Diana's journey was filled with ups and downs—moments of financial success followed by unexpected setbacks. She had to learn how to navigate these fluctuations without losing sight of her long-term goals.

Simba, a young man from Zimbabwe, arrived in Australia full of hope and ambition. But the reality of managing his finances in a new country soon hit him hard. Between paying off student loans, covering living expenses, and trying to build an emergency fund, Simba found himself overwhelmed by debt. It felt like no matter how hard he worked, he couldn't get ahead.

Ava, originally from Rwanda, had always been a planner. She knew that if she wanted to retire comfortably and leave a legacy for her family, she needed to start planning early. But life had other plans, and Ava faced a series of financial setbacks that made her question whether she would ever achieve her dreams. From unemployment to unexpected medical expenses, Ava had to navigate a maze of challenges to stay on track with her financial goals.

These six individuals faced different financial challenges, but they all had one thing in common: the determination to overcome them. Their stories highlight some of the most common financial challenges that many people face, regardless of background or circumstance.

9.1.1 Managing Debt: A Heavy Burden

For John, managing debt was like trying to climb out of a deep hole with no ladder. Every time he made progress, another unexpected expense or interest charge would set him back. He knew that he needed to take control of his debt if he was ever going to provide the life he wanted for his family. John learned that the first step to managing debt was understanding it—knowing what he owed, the interest rates, and the minimum payments. By creating a debt repayment plan, John was able to prioritize his debts and start making more than the minimum payments on his highest-interest loans.

Simba faced a similar challenge. He had accumulated debt during his studies and was now working to pay it off. But the weight of that debt felt suffocating. Simba knew he needed to make changes, so he sought advice from a financial counselor. Together, they developed a strategy to tackle his debt, starting with creating a budget that allowed him to allocate extra funds toward his repayments. Slowly but surely, Simba began to see progress, and with each payment, he felt a little more free.

9.1.2 Dealing with Unexpected Expenses: The Unseen Storms

Unexpected expenses can be one of the most destabilizing financial challenges. For Faith, the unpredictability of life as a single mother meant that she always had to be prepared for the unexpected. Whether it was a trip to the emergency room for her son or a broken-down car, Faith knew that one unplanned expense could derail her entire budget. She learned the hard way that having an emergency fund was essential. By setting aside even a small amount of money each month, Faith was able to build a financial cushion that gave her peace of mind.

Diana also faced unexpected expenses that tested her financial resilience. She had been doing well, steadily building her savings, when a series of medical bills suddenly wiped out much of her progress. It was a frustrating setback, but Diana refused to let it derail her long-term plans. She adjusted her budget, focused on rebuilding her emergency fund, and took it one step at a time.

9.1.3 Planning for Life Changes: Adapting to the Unexpected

Life is full of changes, and being financially prepared for those changes is crucial. Deng faced several life changes that required him to adapt his financial plans. As he transitioned from being a student to working full-time, Deng realized that his financial responsibilities were shifting. No longer just providing for himself, Deng had to think about supporting his family back home while also building his own future in Australia. This meant making tough decisions about how to allocate his income and finding a balance between his short-term needs and long-term goals.

Ava, too, experienced significant life changes that affected her financial plans. When she lost her job unexpectedly, Ava was forced to reassess her financial situation. With her retirement goals still in sight, she had to make difficult choices about how to manage her superannuation and savings while looking for new employment. Ava's story highlights the importance of being adaptable and having a financial plan that can withstand life's ups and downs.

9.2 Strategies for Overcoming Financial Challenges: The Path Forward

Each of these individuals faced significant financial challenges, but they didn't let those challenges define them. Instead, they developed strategies to overcome their obstacles and create a more secure financial future. The following strategies are drawn from their experiences and can be applied to your own financial journey.

9.2.1 Creating a Financial Plan: A Roadmap to Success

Faith's journey taught her the importance of having a financial plan. As a single mother, she needed a roadmap to navigate the complexities of managing her household on one income. Faith started by setting financial goals—both short-term and long-term—and developing a budget that reflected her priorities. She used financial planning software to track her expenses and monitor her progress, making adjustments along the way.

Ava also relied on a financial plan to keep her focused on her retirement goals. Despite the setbacks she faced, Ava never lost sight of her vision for the future. By setting clear goals, regularly reviewing her progress, and staying disciplined in her approach, Ava was able to stay on track and make informed decisions about her finances.

9.2.2 Building Financial Resilience: Weathering the Storms

Building financial resilience means being prepared for the unexpected and having the flexibility to adapt when things don't go according to plan. For Simba, building resilience meant diversifying his income sources and improving his financial literacy. He took on side jobs to increase his income and attended workshops to learn more about managing his money. These efforts not only helped Simba pay off his debt but also gave him the confidence to navigate future financial challenges.

Diana's resilience was tested when she faced unexpected medical expenses. But instead of letting those expenses derail her progress, she used the experience as an opportunity to strengthen her financial safety nets. By rebuilding her emergency fund and reviewing her insurance coverage, Diana ensured that she would be better prepared for any future setbacks.

9.2.3 Utilizing Financial Resources: Support When You Need It

One of the most important lessons that these individuals learned was the value of seeking help when needed. Whether it was financial assistance programs, community organizations, or professional advisors, each of them found support that helped them navigate their financial challenges.

Deng, for example, accessed scholarships and financial aid programs during his studies, which allowed him to continue pursuing his education without overwhelming debt. Faith, on the other hand, turned to government programs that provided financial assistance for single mothers. These resources were lifelines during difficult times and helped them stay on course.

9.3 Planning for the Future: Securing What Matters Most

Planning for the future isn't just about addressing immediate financial challenges—it's about creating a foundation for long-term success. Each of these individuals recognized the importance of planning for their future, whether it was saving for retirement, investing in education, or building a legacy for their loved ones.

9.3.1 Long-Term Financial Goals: Investing in the Future

Ava's focus on retirement planning demonstrates the power of setting long-term financial goals. She knew from the start that securing her retirement would require more than just saving money—it required a commitment to making wise investments and regularly reviewing her superannuation strategy. Despite the setbacks she encountered along the way, Ava remained dedicated to her goals. She met with financial advisors, diversified her investments, and made voluntary contributions to her superannuation. These steps ensured that her retirement fund grew steadily, providing her with peace of mind as she approached her later years.

Simba also had long-term goals, but for him, it was about building a financial safety net to support his family back in Zimbabwe. He started investing small amounts into various assets, including property and shares, aiming to create a portfolio that would not only generate income but also grow over time. Simba's story illustrates that no matter your circumstances, having a vision for your future can help you stay motivated and make decisions that align with your long-term objectives.

Deng, after his initial struggle to balance his education and financial responsibilities, realized the importance of setting a solid foundation for his future. He wanted to provide not just for his family back home, but also for himself in the long run. Deng began to see his savings and investments as a bridge to future opportunities—whether that meant buying a home, furthering his education, or starting a business. He knew that with careful planning and consistent effort, he could turn his financial dreams into reality.

9.3.2 Financial Safety Nets: Protecting What You've Built

Life is unpredictable, and the ability to weather financial storms is crucial for long-term stability. Faith's experience as a single mother taught her that having financial safety nets in place—like an emergency fund and adequate insurance coverage—could make all the difference in times of crisis. By setting aside a portion of her income for emergencies, Faith was able to handle unexpected expenses without resorting to debt or compromising her long-term goals.

John also came to understand the importance of financial safety nets after facing his own challenges with debt. Once he regained control of his finances, John focused on building a cushion to protect his family from future financial hardships. He increased his savings, reviewed his insurance policies, and made sure his family was covered in case of any unforeseen events. This proactive approach gave John peace of mind and allowed him to focus on building a brighter future for his loved ones.

9.3.3 Estate Planning: Leaving a Legacy

For Ava, estate planning was about more than just ensuring her assets would be distributed according to her wishes—it was about leaving a legacy that would continue to benefit her family for generations to come. She worked with an estate planner to create a will, designate beneficiaries, and set up trusts that would provide for her siblings and their children. Ava knew that the financial security she had worked so hard to build could be a lasting gift to her family, helping them achieve their own dreams even after she was gone.

Diana, too, recognized the importance of estate planning as she approached her 30s. After years of hard work and dedication, she had built a modest but growing portfolio of assets. Diana wanted to ensure that her wealth would be used to support her family and future generations. She began working with a financial advisor to develop an estate plan that would protect her assets and allow her to pass on her legacy with confidence.

Estate planning wasn't just about the future for these individuals—it was about creating a lasting impact on the people they cared about. By taking the time to plan for the future, they were able to ensure that their hard-earned wealth would continue to provide for their loved ones, even after they were gone.

9.4 Resources and Tools: Empowering Financial Growth

No one navigates financial challenges alone, and each of these characters sought out resources and tools to help them along the way. From financial planning software to community organizations, they made use of the support available to them, which ultimately helped them achieve their financial goals.

9.4.1 Financial Planning Software: A Helping Hand in Organizing Finances

Faith found budgeting apps and financial planning software to be indispensable tools in managing her finances as a single mother. These tools allowed her to track her income and expenses, set savings goals, and monitor her progress. They provided structure and clarity, helping her stay on top of her financial responsibilities without feeling overwhelmed.

Deng also turned to financial software to manage his growing responsibilities. With the help of these tools, he was able to track his earnings, set aside money for his family back home, and allocate funds toward his own goals in Australia. These tools gave Deng the confidence to make informed decisions and stay on track with his financial plan.

9.4.2 Financial Assistance Resources: Reaching Out for Support

Simba's journey was made easier by accessing financial assistance resources available in his community. Whether it was credit counseling services or government programs, these resources provided Simba with the guidance and support he needed to tackle his debt and build a more stable financial future. Similarly, John found relief through debt relief services, which helped him consolidate his debts and develop a repayment plan that worked for his family.

Diana also took advantage of financial literacy programs offered by local community groups. These programs gave her the knowledge and confidence to make better financial decisions, and she used that knowledge to build a strong financial foundation for herself and her future family.

9.4.3 Professional Advisors: The Value of Expert Guidance

Each of these individuals recognized the value of seeking professional advice at various stages of their financial journey. Ava worked closely with financial planners and estate advisors to ensure that her retirement and estate plans were aligned with her long-term goals. Simba sought out financial counseling to help him navigate his debt, while Diana consulted with investment advisors to maximize her savings and build a diverse portfolio.

John and Deng, too, benefited from expert guidance, whether through financial coaching or legal advice. These professional advisors provided the expertise and insight needed to make informed decisions and avoid costly mistakes. Their guidance allowed each individual to move forward with confidence, knowing that their financial plans were built on a solid foundation.

Conclusion: Strength Through Challenges, Hope for the Future

The stories of Deng, John, Faith, Diana, Simba, and Ava are not just tales of financial challenges—they are stories of resilience, hope, and growth. Each of these individuals faced significant obstacles, but through careful planning, resourcefulness, and the support of their communities, they were able to overcome those challenges and build a brighter future.

Their journeys teach us that financial stability isn't about perfection—it's about persistence. It's about recognizing that setbacks are a part of life and that with the right strategies, support, and mindset, we can navigate those setbacks and come out stronger on the other side.

Whether it's managing debt, dealing with unexpected expenses, or planning for retirement, the lessons learned by these individuals are universally applicable. They remind us that financial challenges don't define us—how we respond to them does.

Lessons for the Readers:

1. **Start Planning Early:** As Ava, Faith, and Deng demonstrated, the earlier you start planning for your financial future, the more time you have to build wealth and secure your goals. Whether you're focusing on retirement, building an emergency fund, or managing debt, starting early gives you the advantage of time and compound growth.

2. **Understand Your Financial Tools:** Superannuation, investments, and estate planning tools are powerful resources for building long-term wealth and protecting your legacy. Like Ava and Diana, it's essential to understand how these tools work and how to maximize their potential to meet your financial goals.

3. **Build Financial Safety Nets:** Life is unpredictable, and financial safety nets like emergency funds and insurance coverage are crucial for weathering storms. Faith and John's experiences show that having these safety nets in place can provide peace of mind and protect your financial stability during difficult times.

4. **Seek Support When Needed:** Don't be afraid to reach out for help when navigating financial challenges. Whether it's community resources, professional advisors, or financial assistance programs, as Simba and John found, seeking support can make all the difference in overcoming obstacles and achieving your financial goals.

5. **Focus on Building a Legacy:** Financial planning isn't just about securing your own future—it's about creating a lasting impact for your loved ones. Ava's careful estate planning ensured that her wealth would continue to benefit her family for generations. Consider how your financial decisions today will shape the future for those you care about.

6. **Stay Resilient and Adaptive:** Life will throw challenges your way, but as Deng and Simba show, resilience and adaptability are key to overcoming those challenges. Stay focused on your goals, be willing to adjust your plans when necessary, and remember that setbacks are not the end—they are opportunities to learn and grow.

Final Thoughts

Navigating financial challenges and planning for the future requires courage, perseverance, and the willingness to seek help when needed. The stories of Deng, John, Faith, Diana, Simba, and Ava remind us that no matter where we start, we all have the power to build a secure and meaningful financial future. It's not about avoiding challenges—it's about facing them head-on, learning from them, and using them as stepping stones toward the life we envision.

As you move forward on your financial journey, remember that you are not alone. The resources, tools, and support you need are out there—reach out, stay resilient, and keep moving toward your goals. With the right mindset and a solid plan, you too can navigate life's financial challenges and create a future filled with hope, security, and success.

CHAPTER 10

FINANCIAL LITERACY FOR THE NEXT GENERATION

Introduction: The Power of Financial Knowledge Across Generations

Deng, Faith, Ava, Simba, and John. Each of them arrived in Australia with dreams of a better life, but all of them faced the stark reality of navigating an entirely new financial system. Along their journeys, they encountered financial challenges, but they also found opportunities to build wealth, provide for their families, and create legacies. Now, as they reflect on their paths, one thing becomes abundantly clear: financial literacy is the key to unlocking the future, not just for themselves but for their children and future generations.

In this chapter, we will explore how the lessons learned from Deng, Faith, Ava, Simba, and John can be passed on to the next generation. We'll delve into why financial literacy is so vital, how to introduce financial concepts early, and the role of parents and guardians in fostering financial independence. We'll also discuss how financial literacy can extend beyond the family and into the community, creating a ripple effect of financial empowerment.

Through practical tips, storytelling, and reflection, this chapter will guide you on how to instill financial knowledge and values in your children and younger family members. By teaching the next generation to navigate the financial world with confidence, we can ensure that they are prepared to face the challenges ahead.

10.1 The Importance of Financial Literacy for Youth

10.1.1 Why Financial Literacy Matters

Financial literacy is not just about understanding how money works—it's about making informed decisions that can shape the course of a person's life. For young people, learning financial literacy early means they can avoid many of the pitfalls that Deng, Faith, Ava, Simba, and John encountered as they tried to build stable lives in a new country.

Story: Deng's Realization of Missed Financial Education

Reflecting on his journey, Deng often thought about how different his early years in Australia would have been if he had known more about money management. He came from a background where financial literacy wasn't taught at home, and the complexity of the Australian financial system overwhelmed him at first. Over time, Deng learned, but he wished he had started much earlier. Now, as a father, he made it his mission to teach his children what he hadn't been taught. By ensuring his children understand budgeting, saving, and investing from a young age, he's giving them a head start that he never had.

10.1.2 The Benefits of Financial Literacy

Teaching financial literacy from a young age has several long-term benefits:

- **Improved Money Management:** Learning how to create a budget, manage expenses, and save for future goals leads to better money management and less financial stress.

- **Reduced Financial Mistakes:** Financial literacy helps young people avoid costly mistakes, such as racking up debt on credit cards or falling victim to financial scams.

- **Long-Term Financial Stability:** By understanding concepts like compound interest, investing, and retirement planning early on, young people can make decisions that lead to long-term financial security.

Deng's experience highlighted the importance of equipping his children with these skills early so they could navigate the financial world with confidence and security.

10.2 Introducing Financial Concepts Early: Building the Foundation

10.2.1 Starting Early: Ages 3-6

At a young age, children are naturally curious and eager to learn. This is the perfect time to introduce basic financial concepts. Faith, who always emphasized the importance of education in her family, found creative ways to teach her young daughter about money.

Faith would use play money and games to teach her daughter about the value of money. For example, they would set up a "store" at home, where Faith's daughter could "buy" toys or snacks with play money. This simple game taught her about the exchange of money for goods, laying the foundation for more complex financial concepts later in life.

10.2.2 Developing Skills: Ages 7-12

As children grow older, they can begin to grasp more complex financial concepts. During this stage, it's important to introduce budgeting, saving, and spending wisely. Ava, who was meticulous about her own financial planning, decided to create a budget with her two nephews. They each received an allowance, and Ava taught them how to divide it into three categories: saving, spending, and sharing.

Through this exercise, Ava's nephews learned that not all money should be spent immediately. They began to understand the importance of setting aside money for future needs and charitable giving. This small but powerful lesson instilled in them the values of responsibility and generosity.

10.2.3 Preparing for Independence: Ages 13-18

In the teenage years, financial education becomes even more critical as young people begin earning their own money through part-time jobs or allowances. Simba, who struggled with debt in his early adulthood, wanted to make sure his teenage son avoided the same mistakes. He sat down with him to explain the importance of credit, how interest rates work, and the dangers of debt.

Simba's son opened his first bank account, and together, they discussed the importance of maintaining a good credit score. Simba emphasized that while credit can be a useful tool, it should be used wisely and with caution. By sharing his own experiences, Simba made the lessons more relatable and impactful.

10.3 Tools and Resources for Financial Education: Making Learning Engaging

The financial world can seem daunting to young people, but with the right tools and resources, financial education can be both engaging and effective.

10.3.1 Educational Games and Apps

For younger children, interactive games and apps can make financial concepts fun and accessible. Apps like PiggyBot and Bankaroo allow children to manage virtual money, set savings goals, and learn the value of budgeting in an age-appropriate way.

For older children and teenagers, apps like Mint and PocketGuard help them track their real-life spending, set budgets, and manage their money independently. These tools make financial education more hands-on and practical, giving young people the opportunity to apply what they've learned in a real-world context.

10.3.2 Books and Educational Materials

Books can be a powerful way to introduce financial concepts. Faith found that reading books like "The Berenstain Bears' Trouble with Money" to her daughter opened up conversations about how money works and why it's important to save.

For teenagers, books like "Rich Dad Poor Dad for Teens" by Robert Kiyosaki provide valuable lessons on entrepreneurship, investing, and financial independence. These books help young readers understand that wealth-building starts with the right mindset and good financial habits.

10.3.3 School Programs and Workshops

Simba recognized the value of community and school-based programs in supplementing what he taught his son at home. Programs like financial literacy workshops or after-school clubs give young people the opportunity to learn from different perspectives and discuss financial topics with their peers.

Encouraging participation in these programs helps solidify the lessons learned at home and provides a broader understanding of financial literacy.

10.4 Creating a Financial Education Plan: Structuring the Learning Process

Financial literacy shouldn't be left to chance. Creating a structured financial education plan helps ensure that children and young adults develop the skills they need to manage their money effectively.

10.4.1 Setting Clear Objectives

John, who was diligent about setting goals for himself and his family, decided to take the same approach with financial education. He created a financial education plan for his children that included clear objectives for each stage of their development.

John started with simple goals, like teaching his children how to budget their allowances, and gradually moved on to more complex concepts like investing and retirement planning as they grew older. By breaking down financial education into manageable steps, John ensured that his children were learning at a pace that made sense for them.

10.4.2 Incorporating Learning into Daily Life

Financial education doesn't have to be confined to formal lessons—it can be incorporated into daily life. Ava often used everyday activities as teaching moments for her nephews. Whether it was grocery shopping, planning a family vacation, or discussing bills, Ava found opportunities to talk about money and how to manage it responsibly.

This approach made financial education feel more natural and relevant. Ava's nephews saw how financial decisions played out in real life, making the lessons more memorable and impactful.

10.4.3 Encouraging Open Communication

Creating an environment where financial topics can be discussed openly is key to effective financial education. Deng, who grew up in a culture where money was rarely talked about, made it a point to have regular family meetings where financial matters were discussed openly.

These meetings allowed Deng's children to ask questions, share their thoughts, and learn from their parents' experiences. By fostering open communication, Deng ensured that his children felt comfortable discussing money and seeking advice when they needed it.

10.5 The Role of Parents and Guardians: Leading by Example

As parents and guardians, we are the first financial teachers our children will have. Our actions, decisions, and attitudes toward money shape their understanding of finances.

10.5.1 Leading by Example

Children learn by watching, and our financial behavior serves as a model for them. Ava made a conscious effort to demonstrate responsible money management to her nephews. She regularly involved them in her budgeting process and explained how she prioritized saving, investing, and giving back to her community.

By seeing Ava's thoughtful approach to money, her nephews learned the value of careful financial planning and the importance of aligning financial decisions with personal values.

10.5.2 Encouraging Independence

Faith believed that financial independence was a gift she could give her daughter. She encouraged her daughter to make her own financial decisions, even if it meant making mistakes along the way. Faith would give her daughter an allowance and let her manage it on her own, offering guidance only when needed. This allowed her daughter to experience the consequences of overspending and the rewards of saving, giving her a hands-on understanding of financial management.

By giving her daughter the freedom to make her own financial choices, Faith empowered her to become financially independent and responsible. She knew that these lessons would serve her daughter well as she grew older and began managing larger amounts of money.

10.5.3 Providing Resources and Support

Simba understood that while it was important to give his son independence, he also needed to provide the right resources and support. He introduced his son to financial tools, such as budgeting apps and online investment platforms, and encouraged him to explore them.

Simba also made sure to be available whenever his son had questions or needed advice. He didn't want his son to feel overwhelmed or alone in his financial journey. By providing both the tools and the support, Simba helped his son build confidence in his ability to manage his finances.

10.6 Financial Literacy Beyond the Family: Empowering Communities

While financial literacy often begins at home, its impact can extend far beyond the immediate family. Deng, Faith, Ava, Simba, and John all understood the importance of sharing their knowledge with others and contributing to the financial literacy of their communities.

10.6.1 Supporting Community Programs

Deng, who had always valued community, decided to volunteer at a local organization that offered financial literacy workshops for new immigrants. He shared his own experiences of navigating the Australian financial system and helped others avoid the mistakes he had made. For Deng, giving back to his community was not only fulfilling but also a way to ensure that more people had access to the knowledge and resources they needed to succeed.

By supporting community programs that promote financial literacy, we can create a ripple effect of empowerment that reaches beyond our own families.

10.6.2 Advocating for Financial Education

Faith became an advocate for financial education in her local school district. She knew that not all children received financial education at home, and she wanted to make sure that schools were stepping in to fill that gap. Faith worked with educators and administrators to develop financial literacy programs that could be integrated into the school curriculum.

By advocating for financial education at the institutional level, Faith helped ensure that more young people in her community would have the opportunity to learn essential financial skills.

10.6.3 Sharing Knowledge with Peers

Ava took a different approach—she started a financial literacy group with her friends and family. They met regularly to discuss various financial topics, such as budgeting, investing, and retirement planning. Ava found that sharing knowledge in a supportive group setting not only helped others but also deepened her own understanding of financial concepts.

Through these discussions, Ava and her peers were able to learn from each other's experiences and make more informed financial decisions. By creating a space for open dialogue about money, Ava helped break down the stigma around financial conversations and empowered others to take control of their finances.

10.7 Creating a Lasting Legacy of Financial Empowerment

Financial literacy is about more than just teaching skills—it's about creating a legacy of empowerment that can be passed down through generations. Deng, Faith, Ava, Simba, and John all understood that by investing in the financial education of their children and communities, they were creating a brighter future for everyone.

10.7.1 Building Financial Confidence

When young people are equipped with financial knowledge, they gain confidence in their ability to manage their money and make informed decisions. This confidence can have a profound impact on their lives, allowing them to pursue their dreams, achieve financial stability, and avoid the stress and uncertainty that comes with financial insecurity.

Faith's daughter, who had learned about money management from an early age, grew up with a strong sense of financial confidence. She knew how to budget, save, and invest, and she felt empowered to make financial decisions that aligned with her goals. This confidence gave her the freedom to pursue her passions without being held back by financial worries.

10.7.2 Creating Financially Independent Adults

One of the greatest gifts we can give the next generation is the ability to stand on their own two feet financially. Simba's son, who had learned about the dangers of debt and the importance of credit, grew up to be a financially independent adult. He managed his finances responsibly, avoided unnecessary debt, and made smart investment decisions that allowed him to build wealth over time.

By teaching young people to be financially independent, we help them build lives of freedom and security. They are not reliant on others for financial support, and they have the tools they need to create the future they want.

10.7.3 Leaving a Legacy of Financial Wisdom

For Deng, Ava, and John, financial literacy was about more than just their own families—it was about leaving a legacy of financial wisdom that would benefit future generations. They knew that by teaching their children and communities about money, they were planting seeds that would grow into a legacy of empowerment.

Deng's children, Ava's nephews, and John's children all carried forward the lessons they had learned, passing them on to their own families and communities. This ripple effect of financial literacy ensured that the knowledge and skills that had been so hard-won would continue to benefit future generations.

Conclusion: Empowering the Next Generation

As we reflect on the journeys of Deng, Faith, Ava, Simba, and John, one thing becomes clear: financial literacy is not just a skill—it's a gift. It's a gift that we can give to our children, our families, and our communities. It's a gift that empowers people to take control of their futures, make informed decisions, and build lives of security and freedom.

By investing in financial literacy for the next generation, we are creating a legacy that will endure for years to come. We are giving young people the tools they need to navigate the financial world with confidence, resilience, and wisdom. We are ensuring that they are prepared for whatever challenges the future may hold and that they have the knowledge and skills to create the lives they want.

The lessons learned from Deng, Faith, Ava, Simba, and John remind us that financial literacy is a journey—a journey that begins with education and continues throughout our lives. As we move forward, let us commit to passing on the knowledge and values that have shaped our own financial journeys. Let us empower the next generation to build a future of financial security, independence, and success.

In the words of Ava, "Financial literacy isn't just about money—it's about freedom. It's about having the freedom to make choices, the freedom to pursue your dreams, and the freedom to build the life you want. That's the legacy I want to leave behind."

Empowering the Future Through Financial Literacy

As we draw this journey to a close, the final chapter encapsulates a central theme that runs throughout this book: the power of financial literacy. We've followed the stories of individuals from various walks of life—Deng, Faith, Ava, Simba, and John—who all embarked on their unique financial journeys. Their stories highlight the importance of understanding money, making informed decisions, and empowering future generations with the knowledge that can transform lives.

Financial literacy is more than just a skill—it's a lifelong journey that begins with education and continues through experience and growth. By focusing on teaching the next generation how to manage money wisely, we are laying the foundation for stronger, more resilient individuals, families, and communities. The lessons learned from the characters in this book are universal and deeply relevant in a world where financial security is key to achieving personal goals, dreams, and stability.

The Power of Financial Literacy

This chapter has emphasized the immense impact financial literacy can have on individuals and communities. It teaches young people how to make wise financial choices, helping them avoid the pitfalls of debt, understand the power of saving and investing, and build a strong foundation for their futures. The benefits of financial literacy are far-reaching:

1. **Empowerment:** Financial literacy empowers individuals to take control of their lives by making informed financial decisions. It helps them navigate the complexities of personal finance, from budgeting and saving to investing and retirement planning.

2. **Stability:** With the right financial knowledge, people can build a safety net that protects them from unexpected life events and economic downturns. Financial stability creates peace of mind and allows individuals to focus on other important areas of their lives.

3. **Legacy:** By teaching financial literacy to the next generation, we ensure that the knowledge and wisdom we've acquired are passed down, helping future generations achieve financial security and independence.

A Call to Action: Start Now, Shape the Future

Financial literacy isn't just something that happens—it's something we actively cultivate. Whether you are a parent, guardian, educator, or community leader, you have the power to make a difference. You can start today by incorporating financial education into everyday conversations, leading by example, and providing resources that will equip the next generation with the knowledge they need to succeed.

Here's how you can take action:

1. **Teach Financial Literacy at Home:** Begin by teaching basic financial concepts to your children or young family members. Start with small lessons on budgeting, saving, and the value of money.

As they grow, introduce more complex topics like investing, credit management, and retirement planning.

2. **Support Financial Education Programs:** Advocate for financial literacy in schools and community organizations. Volunteer your time or resources to support programs that aim to educate young people about personal finance.

3. **Lead by Example:** Your financial habits will serve as a model for others, especially the younger generation. Make responsible financial decisions, openly discuss money matters, and show how thoughtful planning can lead to financial success.

4. **Encourage Open Conversations:** Break the stigma around talking about money. Encourage open, honest conversations about financial goals, challenges, and strategies within your family and community. The more we talk about money, the less intimidating it becomes.

Key Learnings from This Chapter

The final chapter has underscored several key learnings that are essential for anyone committed to fostering financial literacy in the next generation:

1. **Start Early:** Financial education should begin as early as possible. Teaching children about money management from a young age helps them develop healthy financial habits that will serve them throughout their lives.

2. **Be Consistent:** Financial literacy is not a one-time lesson; it requires ongoing education and reinforcement. Regularly revisit financial topics as children grow and as their understanding deepens.

3. **Use Real-Life Examples:** Practical, real-world examples make financial concepts easier to grasp. Use everyday situations to teach lessons about budgeting, saving, and making financial decisions.

4. **Empower Independence:** Give young people the freedom to manage their money and make decisions—both good and bad. Experience is a powerful teacher, and financial independence is a skill that can only be developed through practice.

5. **Create a Financial Education Plan:** Develop a structured plan to guide financial education in your home or community. Set clear objectives, use the right tools, and ensure that learning is a continuous process.

6. **Think Beyond the Individual:** Financial literacy has the potential to transform not just individuals but entire communities. By supporting financial education initiatives, we can create a ripple effect that benefits society as a whole.

A Legacy of Empowerment

As you reflect on this final chapter, remember that financial literacy is about more than just managing money—it's about creating opportunities, building a better future, and leaving a lasting legacy. Deng, Faith, Ava, Simba, and John all found success not just in achieving their own financial goals but in passing on their knowledge to others. Their stories remind us that financial education is a powerful tool for creating change, both within our own lives and within our communities.

Let this book be a call to action. Start the conversation about financial literacy today. Educate yourself, your children, and your community. Empower others to take control of their financial futures. Together, we can build a world where financial literacy is not just a privilege but a right—where every individual has the knowledge and tools they need to achieve financial security and success.

The future is in our hands. Let's shape it wisely.

Appendices

The appendices provide essential tools, resources, and additional guidance to help you implement the strategies outlined in *From Ground Up: A Financial Empowerment for African Migrants in Australia.* These resources are designed to be practical and accessible, complementing the insights shared in the main chapters. Whether you're new to financial planning or seeking advanced strategies, these appendices offer the support you need to take action and move closer to your financial goals.

Appendix A: Financial Calculators and Tools

The financial calculators below are designed to make budgeting, loan management, and savings planning easier. Use them as a starting point to take control of your finances.

1. **Budgeting Calculator**

Purpose: Helps you plan your monthly finances by tracking income, expenses, and savings, ensuring your budget supports your financial goals.

How to Use:
- Input your total monthly income.
- List all fixed expenses (e.g., rent, utilities) and variable expenses (e.g., groceries, entertainment).
- Calculate the difference between income and expenses.
- Adjust spending or savings goals as needed to balance your budget.

Example:

Category	Amount ($)
Income	4,000
Rent/Mortgage	1,200
Utilities	200
Groceries	300
Transportation	150
Savings	250
Entertainment	100
Total Expenses	2,200
Remaining Balance	1,800

2. Loan Repayment Calculator

Purpose: Estimate monthly payments for loans, including mortgages, personal loans, and student loans. This tool helps you understand the total cost of borrowing and manage debt effectively.

How to Use:

- Enter the loan amount.

- Specify the interest rate and loan term.

- Calculate the monthly payment and the total interest paid over the life of the loan.

Example:

Loan Amount ($)	Interest Rate (%)	Term (Years)	Monthly Payment ($)	Total Interest Paid ($)
20,000	5	5	377	2,619

3. **Savings Goal Calculator**

Purpose: Helps you break down larger savings goals into manageable monthly contributions, ensuring you stay on track to achieve your financial objectives.

How to Use:

- Define your savings goal amount.

- Set a target date for achieving the goal.

- Calculate the monthly savings required to reach the goal by the target date.

Example:

Goal Amount ($)	Target Date	Monthly Savings Required ($)
5,000	12 months	417

Appendix B: Sample Budget Templates

To effectively manage your finances, use the following templates for monthly and annual budgeting. These tools will help you plan your income, control expenses, and achieve your financial goals.

1. Monthly Budget Template

Purpose: Provides a structured format for tracking your income, expenses, and savings each month. Regularly updating your budget helps you make adjustments as needed.

Template:

Category	Budgeted Amount ($)	Actual Amount ($)	Difference ($)
Income			
Fixed Expenses			
Variable Expenses			
Savings			
Total			

2. Annual Budget Template

Purpose: Use this template to plan and track your income and expenses over the course of an entire year. This long-term perspective helps you better manage larger financial goals, such as saving for a home, investing, or retirement planning.

Template:

Category	Annual Budgeted Amount ($)	Annual Actual Amount ($)	Difference ($)
Income			
Fixed Expenses			
Variable Expenses			
Savings			
Total			

Appendix C: Investment Glossary

Investing can be intimidating, especially for those new to the financial world. The following glossary provides clear definitions of key investment terms and concepts to help you feel more confident in your investment decisions.

1. **Key Investment Terms**
   - **Asset Allocation:** Dividing investments among different categories (e.g., stocks, bonds, real estate) to manage risk and achieve financial goals.

   - **Diversification:** Spreading investments across various asset classes to reduce risk and minimize the impact of poor performance in any one area.

   - **Dividend:** A distribution of a portion of a company's earnings to its shareholders, often paid out in cash or additional shares.

   - **Mutual Fund:** An investment fund that pools money from multiple investors to purchase a diversified portfolio of securities, managed by professionals.

   - **Risk Tolerance:** The level of uncertainty in investment returns that an investor is comfortable with.

   - **Return on Investment (ROI):** A measure of the profitability of an investment, calculated as the ratio of gain or loss to the initial investment amount.

2. **Common Financial Ratios**
   - **Price-to-Earnings (P/E) Ratio:** A valuation ratio that compares a company's current share price to its earnings per share (EPS). A higher ratio may indicate that a stock is overvalued.

- **Debt-to-Equity Ratio:** A measure of a company's financial leverage, showing the proportion of debt used to finance assets relative to shareholders' equity.

- **Current Ratio:** A liquidity ratio that assesses a company's ability to pay off its short-term liabilities with its short-term assets.

3. **Glossary of Banking Terms**
   - **Overdraft:** A facility allowing an account holder to withdraw more money than is available in their account, up to an agreed limit, typically with interest charges.

   - **Term Deposit:** A savings account where funds are locked in for a fixed term at a set interest rate, often offering higher returns than regular savings accounts.

   - **Interest Rate:** The percentage charged or earned on borrowed or invested money, respectively.

Appendix D: Additional Reading and Resources

Financial education is a lifelong journey. The following books, online resources, and tools will help deepen your understanding of personal finance and guide you as you continue your financial journey in Australia.

1. **Books on Financial Literacy**
   - **"The Barefoot Investor" by Scott Pape:** An Australian classic that provides practical, no-nonsense advice on budgeting, saving, and investing.

   - **"Rich Dad Poor Dad" by Robert T. Kiyosaki:** A global bestseller that contrasts the money philosophies of two father figures and provides insights on wealth-building and financial independence.

- **"The Millionaire Next Door" by Thomas J. Stanley and William D. Danko:** A deep dive into the habits of wealthy individuals and what it takes to achieve financial success.

2. **Online Resources**
   - **Australian Securities and Investments Commission (ASIC):** www.asic.gov.au - Offers comprehensive information on financial products, services, and investor protection.
   - **MoneySmart by ASIC:** www.moneysmart.gov.au - A valuable resource for managing money, budgeting, and making informed financial decisions.

3. **Financial Planning Tools**
   - **Personal Finance Apps:** Tools like Mint, YNAB (You Need A Budget), and PocketGuard are excellent for managing your budget, tracking spending, and achieving your financial goals.
   - **Investment Tracking Tools:** Morningstar and Sharesight offer investment tracking and analysis, making it easier to monitor the performance of your portfolio.

Conclusion

These appendices are designed to give you the practical tools and knowledge to take control of your financial future. From tracking your spending to planning for long-term goals, these resources complement the main chapters of the book and provide actionable support as you navigate your financial journey in Australia.

Glossary of Financial Terms

Asset Allocation: The strategy of distributing investments across different asset categories, such as stocks, bonds, and real estate, to manage risk and optimize returns. Asset allocation helps balance risk and reward based on an investor's financial goals, risk tolerance, and investment timeline. For African migrants, understanding asset allocation is crucial for building a diversified portfolio that can weather market fluctuations while steadily growing wealth.

Bond: A debt security where the investor lends money to a borrower, typically a corporation or government, in exchange for periodic interest payments and the return of the principal amount at maturity. Bonds are considered lower risk than stocks but offer lower potential returns. They can be a stable component of a well-rounded investment strategy, particularly for those seeking steady income.

Capital Gains: The profit realized when an asset, such as stocks or real estate, is sold for a price higher than its purchase price. Capital gains are subject to taxation, which can vary depending on how long the asset was held before selling. For new investors, understanding capital gains is key to making informed decisions about when to buy and sell investments.

Credit Score: A numerical rating that reflects an individual's creditworthiness based on their credit history, including borrowing and repayment behavior. Lenders use credit scores to assess the risk of lending money to borrowers. A strong credit score is essential for accessing loans, mortgages, and other financial products at favorable terms, making it a crucial part of financial empowerment for African migrants.

Diversification: The practice of spreading investments across various asset classes, industries, or geographic regions to reduce risk. Diversification ensures that poor performance in one area does not disproportionately affect the overall portfolio. For migrants building their financial future, diversification offers protection against market volatility while increasing potential returns.

Dividend: A portion of a company's earnings distributed to shareholders, typically in cash or additional shares. Dividends are a source of passive income for investors and can be a key component of a long-term wealth-building strategy. For those investing in Australian companies, dividends also offer potential tax benefits through the franking credit system.

Equity: The ownership interest in an asset, such as a business or property, after subtracting liabilities. In the context of investing, equity represents ownership of shares in a company. Building equity, whether in real estate or stocks, is an important step in accumulating wealth over time.

Exchange-Traded Fund (ETF): An investment fund traded on stock exchanges, similar to individual stocks. ETFs typically track an index, sector, or commodity, offering investors diversification and liquidity. ETFs are a popular choice for migrants looking to invest in a diversified portfolio with lower fees and easier access than traditional mutual funds.

Fixed Interest: Investment income that remains constant, such as interest payments from bonds or fixed deposits. Fixed interest investments provide predictable returns and are often used to balance riskier investments like stocks. They are particularly valuable for those nearing retirement or seeking to preserve capital.

Gross Domestic Product (GDP): The total monetary value of all goods and services produced within a country during a specific period. GDP is a key indicator of a nation's economic health and is used to assess growth, stability, and overall performance. Understanding GDP trends can help migrants make informed decisions about their investments and economic participation in Australia.

Inflation: The rate at which the general level of prices for goods and services rises over time, decreasing the purchasing power of money. Inflation affects everything from day-to-day expenses to long-term investments. Planning for inflation is essential in maintaining the value of savings and ensuring that retirement funds last.

Interest Rate: The percentage charged by a lender or earned on an investment. Interest rates can be fixed or variable and have a significant impact on borrowing costs, savings growth, and investment returns. Understanding interest rates is critical for making informed decisions about loans, savings accounts, and investments.

Liability: A financial obligation or debt owed by an individual or organization. Liabilities include loans, mortgages, and other commitments that require repayment. Effective management of liabilities is essential for maintaining financial health and avoiding over-indebtedness.

Mutual Fund : An investment vehicle that pools money from multiple investors to purchase a diversified portfolio of securities, such as stocks, bonds, or real estate. Managed by professionals, mutual funds offer diversification and access to a broad range of assets. For those new to investing, mutual funds provide an opportunity to participate in the market with lower risk.

Net Worth: The total value of an individual's assets minus their liabilities. Net worth is a measure of financial health and can help individuals track their progress toward financial goals. For migrants building a new life in Australia, increasing net worth is a key step toward long-term stability and prosperity.

Portfolio: A collection of investments owned by an individual or institution. Managing a portfolio involves balancing risk and reward to meet specific financial objectives. A well-constructed portfolio is essential for achieving goals like buying a home, funding education, or securing retirement.

Principal: The original amount of money invested or borrowed, excluding interest or earnings. In loans, principal refers to the amount borrowed, while in investments, it refers to the initial capital. Understanding principal is important in calculating returns and managing debt repayments.

Risk Tolerance: An individual's capacity and willingness to endure fluctuations in investment returns. Risk tolerance is influenced by factors such as financial goals, time horizon, and comfort with uncertainty. Recognizing your risk tolerance is essential for making investment decisions that align with your long-term financial plan.

Savings Account: A bank account that earns interest on deposited funds. Savings accounts offer security and liquidity, making them a suitable option for short-term financial goals and emergency funds. While interest rates are typically low, savings accounts provide a safe place to store money with minimal risk.

Stock: A share of ownership in a company, representing a claim on its assets and earnings. Stocks are traded on stock exchanges and can provide returns through dividends and capital gains. Owning stocks is a key component of building wealth and participating in the growth of the economy.

Term Deposit: A fixed-term investment offered by banks where money is locked in for a set period at a predetermined interest rate. Term deposits offer guaranteed returns with minimal risk but may incur penalties for early withdrawal. They are a good option for individuals seeking secure, low-risk investments.

Volatility : The degree of price fluctuation in an asset or market over time. High volatility indicates larger swings in price and increased uncertainty, while low volatility suggests stability. Understanding volatility helps investors manage risk and avoid emotional decision-making during market fluctuations.

Yield: The income generated from an investment, expressed as a percentage of the investment's current value or principal amount. Yield can come from interest payments, dividends, or capital gains. Calculating yield helps investors assess the performance of their investments and make informed choices about where to allocate resources.

ABOUT THE AUTHOR:

YONG DENG DAU

I am Yong Deng Dau, and my story begins in South Sudan. Like many of you, I know the weight of dreams carried across continents, and the determination it takes to rebuild a life in a new country. Arriving in Australia as a young migrant, I faced the complexities of navigating an unfamiliar system, not just for myself, but for my family and my future. Today, I stand as a financial professional and passionate advocate for financial literacy, ready to share what I've learned to empower others to achieve their financial goals.

A Journey Fueled by Resilience and Purpose

My journey in Australia wasn't straightforward. It was shaped by challenges that tested my resolve, but also by opportunities that deepened my understanding of what it takes to succeed financially in a new country. The path I took led me to the world of Banking and Financial Services, where I found my passion for helping others achieve financial security. I started in Home and Business Lending roles, where I saw firsthand the transformative power of financial decisions. This experience sparked a lifelong commitment to demystifying finance for those who, like me, needed guidance.

Over the past decade, I have continued to grow and evolve, working in roles as a Financial Analyst and now as a Consultant in Data and Analytics at one of Australia's top four banks. Each role has deepened my expertise and broadened my perspective, allowing me to blend traditional financial strategies with modern data-driven insights.

A Commitment to Empowering Others

But my work isn't just about finance—it's about empowerment. As someone who had to navigate the complexities of the Australian financial system from the ground up, I understand the fears, frustrations, and uncertainties that many African migrants face. This understanding drives me to make financial knowledge accessible and actionable, especially for those who feel overwhelmed by the challenges of adapting to a new country.

Educational Background and Continuous Growth

My formal education began with a degree in Finance and Accounting, laying the foundation for my career. But I knew that in an ever-evolving financial landscape, continuous learning was key. I pursued advanced studies in Analytics and Machine Learning, equipping myself with the skills to navigate the complexities of the modern financial world. This combination of education and experience allows me to offer insights that are both practical and forward-thinking.

Engagement with the Community

Beyond my professional roles, I am deeply committed to giving back to the community that welcomed me. I work closely with organizations like the African Communities Council of Australia, leading workshops and seminars that help migrants build their financial literacy. My goal is to ensure that others have the knowledge and support they need to thrive in their new home. The work I do in the community is an extension of my personal mission to empower others, one informed decision at a time.

"From Ground Up": A Reflection of My Journey

"From Ground Up: A Financial Empowerment for African Migrants in Australia" is more than just a book—it's a reflection of my own journey. It's a guide born from the lessons I've learned, the mistakes I've made, and the successes I've achieved. Through these pages, I aim to share not only financial strategies but also the hope and resilience that have been the cornerstone of my journey. The stories of individuals like Deng, John, Ava, and others in this book are a testament to the strength and perseverance that define our community.

Looking Ahead

This book is the beginning of a conversation—a conversation about taking control of your financial future, overcoming obstacles, and building a life of security and prosperity in Australia. My hope is that "From Ground Up" serves as a roadmap, guiding you through the complexities of the financial system and empowering you to make informed decisions.

Final Thoughts

Your financial journey is uniquely yours, but you don't have to navigate it alone. I wrote this book to be a companion on your path, offering guidance, support, and practical tools to help you succeed. My story, like yours, is one of resilience, determination, and growth. Together, we can build a strong financial foundation from the ground up—one that supports not just ourselves, but our families and future generations.

Thank you for allowing me to be part of your journey. Here's to building a brighter financial future, together.

With deepest gratitude,
Yong Deng Dau |||